Making a Life

Making a Life

Catholic Social Teaching and the Meaning of Work

Kate Ward

NEW YORK • LONDON • OXFORD • NEW DELHI • SYDNEY

T&T CLARK

Bloomsbury Publishing Inc, 1359 Broadway, New York, NY 10018, USA
Bloomsbury Publishing Plc, 50 Bedford Square, London, WC1B 3DP, UK
Bloomsbury Publishing Ireland, 29 Earlsfort Terrace, Dublin 2, D02 AY28, Ireland

BLOOMSBURY, T&T CLARK and the T&T Clark logo are trademarks of
Bloomsbury Publishing Plc

First published in the United States of America 2026

Copyright © Kate Ward, 2026

Cover design: Diana Nuhn

All rights reserved. No part of this publication may be: i) reproduced or transmitted in any form, electronic or mechanical, including photocopying, recording or by means of any information storage or retrieval system without prior permission in writing from the publishers; or ii) used or reproduced in any way for the training, development or operation of artificial intelligence (AI) technologies, including generative AI technologies. The rights holders expressly reserve this publication from the text and data mining exception as per Article 4(3) of the Digital Single Market Directive (EU) 2019/790.

Bloomsbury Publishing Inc does not have any control over, or responsibility for, any third-party websites referred to or in this book. All internet addresses given in this book were correct at the time of going to press. The author and publisher regret any inconvenience caused if addresses have changed or sites have ceased to exist, but can accept no responsibility for any such changes.

Library of Congress Cataloging-in-Publication Data
Names: Ward, Kate, 1983- author
Title: Making a Life: Catholic Social Teaching and
the Meaning of Work / Kate Ward.
Description: New York: T&T Clark, 2026. |
Includes bibliographical references and index.
Identifiers: LCCN 2025036097 | ISBN 9780567726933 hardback |
ISBN 9780567726926 paperback | ISBN 9780567726940 epub |
ISBN 9780567726957 pdf
Subjects: LCSH: Work–Religious aspects–Catholic Church |
Work–Social aspects–United States
Classification: LCC BX1795.W67 W37 2026
LC record available at https://lccn.loc.gov/2025036097

ISBN: HB: 978-0-5677-2693-3
PB: 978-0-5677-2692-6
ePDF: 978-0-5677-2695-7
eBook: 978-0-5677-2694-0

Typeset by Deanta Global Publishing Services, Chennai, India
Printed and bound in the United States of America

For product safety related questions contact productsafety@bloomsbury.com.

To find out more about our authors and books visit www.bloomsbury.com and sign up for our newsletters.

For Malcolm
with endless love

Contents

Acknowledgements viii
Catholic Social Teaching Documents and Abbreviations x

1 Introduction 1

2 Making a Life: Work and Human Purpose 19

3 Caregiving: Is It Work If You Love Them? 41

4 Drudgery and Flow: The Labor of Food 63

5 Do Artists Work? Creativity and Leisure 95

6 Making a Living: Just Work and Fair Pay 119

7 Building Work We Can Live With 143

Discussion Questions 159
Glossary 168
Index 173

Acknowledgements

This book was completed on a sabbatical from my teaching duties at Marquette University. I am grateful to Marquette's leadership for their support of faculty research, and particularly to my colleagues in the Theology Department, under the able chairships of Conor Kelly and Ryan Duns. Heidi Bostic supported my sabbatical as dean and led discussion groups on Catholic anthropology and leisure which were fertile ground for this book's creation. Most directly, this book grew out of conversations with many Marquette students about Catholic social teaching and the meaning of work. Without their honesty, thoughtfulness, good humor, and willingness to challenge their instructor and our readings, this book would have far less to offer.

I was grateful to complete this book while serving as a Faculty Scholar at the Grefenstette Center for Ethics in Science, Technology and Law at Duquesne University. Thanks to John Slattery and Mia Briceño for enabling a space of rich and gracious conversation and to my fellow Faculty Scholars for so many generative insights. Thanks, also, to the members of the Women in Theology research group, housed at Saint Mary's College in Indiana and directed by Julia Feder, for their generous feedback on an early chapter.

Dedicated research time for tenured faculty is enabled by the labor of contingent faculty colleagues who do the same work without the protections of tenure or the possibility of time off for their own research. During the time I worked on this book, those colleagues included Andrew Blosser, Christina Bosserman, Mark Chapman, Christine Dalessio, Chris Gooding, Jennifer Henery, Matthew Kemp, Sean Larsen, Kathleen McNutt, Jon Metz, Matthew Neujahr, and David Stosur. I am grateful for the many gifts they share with our department as instructors, colleagues and friends. My colleagues in AAUP and Our Marquette have restored my hope more times than I can count.

Acknowledgements

Richard Brown championed this project from the beginning and suggested the perfect title. From publisher to publisher, it's been a delight to work with Tori Shi.

Immense gratitude to the artists who generously answered my questions about their work: Adebisi Agoro, Matthew Bailey, Nick Garcia, Anja Notanja Sieger, Heidi Parkes, and Snežana Žabić. I am in awe of their creativity and passion.

My journey of understanding work winds through Working America, a project of the AFL-CIO, and AFSCME Council 31. Union organizers—those who bravely form and maintain unions at their own workplaces, and the professionals who devote their lives to safer, fairer paid work for others—are my heroes.

My parents, Deborah and Robert Ward, and in-laws, Bob and Chris Filipowicz, generously share the labor of love that is child-raising as well as their experiences as workers and defenders of workers' rights.

Matthew Filipowicz, what I've learned from you about the meaning of work is on every page of this book. How lucky I am to witness your work as an artist, father and community leader. Malcolm, you never cease to bring your family joy. This book is dedicated to you. I love you both so much!

Catholic Social Teaching Documents and Abbreviations

All documents can be accessed online at vatican.va.

Documents of Popes and Church Councils

Leo XIII

RN "Rerum Novarum: On Capital and Labor." May 15, 1891.

Pius XI

QA "Quadragesimo Anno: On Reconstruction of the Social Order." May 15, 1931.

John XXIII

MM "Mater et Magistra: On Christianity and Social Progress." May 15, 1961.

Vatican Council II

GS "Gaudium et Spes: Pastoral Constitution on the Church in the Modern World." December 7, 1965.

Paul VI

PP "Populorum Progressio: On the Development of Peoples." March 26, 1967.

John Paul II

LE   "Laborem Exercens: On Human Work." September 14, 1981.

FC   "Familiaris Consortio: On the Role of the Christian Family in the Modern World." November 22, 1981.

SRS   "Sollicitudo Rei Socialis: On Social Concern." December 30, 1987.

CA   "Centesimus Annus: On the Hundredth Anniversary of Rerum Novarum." May 1, 1991.

DD   "Dies Domini: On Keeping the Lord's Day Holy." May 31, 1998.

Benedict XVI

CV   "Caritas in Veritate: Charity in Truth." June 29, 2009.

Francis

EG   "Evangelii Gaudium: The Joy of the Gospel." November 24, 2013.

LS'   "Laudato Si': On Care for Our Common Home." May 24, 2015.

AL   "Amoris Laetitia: On Love in the Family." March 19, 2016.

FT   "Fratelli Tutti: On Fraternity and Social Friendship." October 3, 2020.

Documents of Vatican Teaching Offices

Pontifical Council for Justice and Peace. "Compendium of the Social Doctrine of the Church." April 2, 2004.

Congregation for the Doctrine of the Faith and Dicastery for Promoting Integral Human Development. "'Oeconomicae et Pecuniariae Quaestiones': Considerations for an Ethical Discernment Regarding Some Aspects of the Present Economic-Financial System." January 6, 2018.

1

Introduction

Chapter Outline

What's Wrong with How We Think about Work Today?	3
The Distinct, Common Worldview behind Catholic Social Teaching	6
What Is Catholic Social Teaching?	10
What to Expect	14

For so many good reasons, people are unhappy with the state of work today. Technology pushes work into ever-expanding areas of our lives, from office workers tied to email at home to truck drivers whose dashboard cams surveil their eye movements. Work takes up more of our time and energy even as we get less out of it. A "risk shift" from employers to workers in recent decades has seen job precarity and economic insecurity increase while healthcare and other benefits have stagnated, resulting in dramatic increases in poor health and early death.[1] Lower-income workers struggle to make ends meet, with millions qualifying for government support even while working full time. Workers at the top of the income spectrum are amassing wealth, but many work in jobs that demand total commitment—zero acknowledgment of family or any life outside work—and are just as vulnerable to layoffs and downsizing as those at lower pay.

Many of us have heard that we should be grateful for a job, grateful for the small percentage we take home of the profits our work generates, and for the shrinking package of benefits some workers earn as part of their compensation. Beyond that, we've heard that we should find a deep sense of meaning and purpose in our paid jobs. And if work interferes with other ways people find meaning and purpose—family, spiritual life, community, and other things we love—we're supposed to accept this as just the way things are. In the United States, many of our public leaders, including Republican and Democratic politicians and major employers, talk about work this way. The writer Derek Thompson dubbed it the new religion of "workism": "the belief that work is not only necessary to economic production, but also the centerpiece of one's identity and life's purpose; and the belief that any policy to promote human welfare must *always* encourage more work."[2] But whether you call it meritocracy or "hustle culture" or just capitalism, this way of thinking about work is sick. It's wrong. It uses an idea—a way of thinking about and understanding work—to pull workers' focus off their compensation and rights, to glamorize work as a passion project rather than an exchange of labor for pay, and to elevate some workers over others, encouraging disrespect for people who do important but unglamorous jobs. This idea about work is hurting you, your community, and your family, if you have one. But we can fix this sorry state of affairs with new ideas about work. Or, actually, with old ones.

The ideas about work I'll outline in this book are rooted in the past and very much alive in the present. For more than 130 years, Catholic popes and bishops have taught an inclusive way of looking at work and its role in our lives that is inspiring and realistic, adaptable to our times, yet rooted in what all humans have in common. It is not a set of policy proposals, but a full worldview of economic activity integrated in communities, rooted in an understanding of what makes a human life worth living. This inclusive vision of work comes from Catholic social teaching, or CST, which some Catholics ruefully call one of the Church's best kept secrets. It is the best framework I know for thinking about what work means, the role you want it to play in your own life, and for developing a shared vision for making work better for everyone.

But wait! you may be saying. Why should I listen to the Catholic Church on work, or on anything? Many of my students have asked the same question. They are not Catholic, or they were raised Catholic but don't accept everything they were taught, or their strongest impression of Catholicism comes from high-profile leaders who spend their time railing against the LGBTQ+ community. For others, coming to understand how many Catholic leaders are implicated in covering up clergy abuse has left the Church completely unacceptable as a moral authority. I understand these reservations and more.

Some Catholics take Catholic social teaching seriously because of who says it. They see the Pope as the preeminent teacher of God's will on earth and know that whoever is the current pope teaches the truth of Catholic belief in continuity with popes before him. For them, any insight emerging from the Catholic tradition, including Catholic social teaching, is self-evidently true because it comes from trusted authorities. Many of the folks who will read this book—including many Catholics—do not have this relationship of unquestioning trust with the Church and those who lead it. People who are not Catholic, or Catholics who disagree with aspects of the Church's teaching or with the way the current Pope communicates the tradition, are never going to welcome Catholic social teaching on the basis of who it comes from. If this describes your feelings, I invite you to give Catholic social teaching a hearing all the same, and to form your opinion not on the basis of who says it, but on the basis of what it says.

What's Wrong with How We Think about Work Today?

In the United States, the mainstream culture around work—"workism"—expects long working hours, high productivity, and a strong connection between work and personal fulfillment, to an extent that is noticeably different than in other wealthy economies. "Workism" has some surprising connections to religious thought. The "Protestant work ethic" was named by sociologist Max Weber, who argued that the Calvinist Protestants whose culture shaped the early United States believed constant economic productivity demonstrated a good relationship with God. Although fewer US people may explicitly believe this now, our culture has fully embraced the idea that economic productivity—or off-the-clock activities that make you more productive, like exercising or studying—is the source of personal dignity and worth. Beyond bestowing dignity, we expect our work to give our lives deep meaning, too.

Many Christians have encountered the idea, first advanced by Martin Luther, that our work can be a "vocation" or a calling from God, not just a job to pay the bills, but a way to live out our deepest purpose on earth. For Luther, this was a transformative way to advocate for the holiness and goodness of ordinary people in a time (and church) that treated priests as inherently superior. The baker, farmer, or homemaker could pursue a path to holiness, toward a God-infused life, in the course of their ordinary activities. The world's Catholic bishops signaled their approval of this insight (only 400-plus years later) when they too taught that earthly activity is a primary way to fulfill our spiritual human "vocation": "Let there be no false opposition between professional and social activities on the one part, and religious life on the other" (*Gaudium et Spes* 43).

A vocational understanding of work reflects human aspirations in important ways. Because we are embodied spirits, what we do all day affects who we become, changing us in ways good or bad. Many people see a good life as one where the work they do all day reflects their values and engages their unique skills, and they hope for such a fit in their own life or their children's future. But this aspiration for paid work to be deeply meaningful can backfire. Critics point out that a paid job giving deep personal meaning may not be realistic or attainable for everyone, and even that some "vocational" understandings of paid work can contribute to exploitative conditions for workers.

Theologian Jon Malesic connects the desire for vocationally fulfilling work to burnout, that "ailment of the soul" that can render us unable to work, paralyzed by "exhaustion, cynicism and despair."[3] Certainly, economic pressures and unrealistic job requirements play a role, but expectations of vocational fulfillment can drive workers to keep pushing themselves beyond what they can take: "We burn out in large part because we believe work is the sure path to social, moral, and spiritual flourishing."[4]

Journalist Sarah Jaffe details how what she calls the "labor-of-love myth" contributes to exploitation in fields ranging from teaching and retail to academia and tech.[5] For Jaffe, the expectation that our work will be done out of love—love for those we serve or for the tasks of the work itself—sets workers up for exploitation by putting the job and its conditions beyond critique. Anne Helen Petersen also critiques cultural pressure to love your job in her widely hailed book *Can't Even: How Millennials Became the Burnout Generation*. Petersen points to the economic context within which millennials (people born in the 1980s, like me) came of age and joined the formal workplace. While earlier generations might more readily have seen employment as a material ticket to survival, millennials absorbed a growing cultural narrative that we should "love" our paid job, an expectation that places immense pressure on workers to find and keep a job that can be worthy of such high fulfillment.[6]

Part of the myth of lovable jobs is that the person who does them is special and uniquely morally praiseworthy. This particular manifestation of workism can drown out our desire to pursue better workplace conditions, even for ourselves, and can erode our solidarity with other workers.[7] Malesic, Petersen, and Jaffe all suggest that the belief that a paid job can be your vocation or something you love sets up a hierarchy of worth between workers who are vocationally "called," or who love what they do, and those who pursue unlovable jobs to pay the bills. Workers who have snagged the elusive, fulfilling, labor-of-love jobs—tenure-track professorships or enviable roles in media—may think they are clearly more deserving than the other workers with the same skills who were not so lucky. And the labor-of-love myth conceals a stark fact that is true for everyone who works for pay: that no matter how we feel about it, a paid job exchanges some of our finite time for resources we need to survive, and the conditions we work in matter a great deal to our own and our family's health and happiness.

If the vocational approach to paid work can lead to burnout and exploitation, the solution isn't to give up on the idea of vocation altogether. The inclusive Catholic definition of work as any purposeful human activity helps us realize that work isn't just our paid job, but all the things we do that make up a life. We can, and should, aspire to vocational fulfillment, pleasure, flow, and all the other good things that work can bring us, but that doesn't mean that a paid job will, or can, provide all those good things.

The religion of "workism" tells us that we're valuable because of what we produce: how much we work, how hard we work, and how effective we manage to be. Catholic social teaching tells us that each of us is inherently valuable and worthy, and that while work is important, we don't earn dignity through our productivity, or in any other way—because you don't have to earn human dignity; it is always already yours. "Workism" tells us that the most important work is the highest paid, and if people can't afford to survive, we need to get them access to more work. (People who can't work, or can't work enough to afford their basic needs? Truth be told, mainstream US work culture doesn't think about them very much.) Catholic social teaching says that everyone has the right to meet their basic needs through work, and if they can't reliably meet basic needs through work, the community has the duty to help them survive just the same.[8]

Increasingly, many people are deciding that workism is not working for them. During the Covid-19 pandemic, we saw large-scale resistance to the status quo in the Great Resignation—when workers left their jobs at unprecedented rates—and trends like "quiet quitting," where young workers online encouraged each other to put in the least effort possible at their paid jobs. Workers organized and joined unions in record numbers after realizing their employers were not looking out for their safety and well-being.[9] Even Pope Francis weighed in, saying that the Great Resignation "does not imply disengagement, but rather the need to humanize work" and recommending that unions could help.[10]

Our dominant culture defines work as what you do for pay. All the other tasks of life—raising your children, caring for your elders or your community, maintaining your health and your home—are not done for pay, so our culture sees them as unimportant, meaning no one but you really cares whether you can manage them along with your paid job. But for Catholic social teaching's inclusive definition of work, your job, your home management, your family and community care—all the things we do that make up a life—are all work. That helps us recognize that things like unpaid family care and self-care are really important, and to see that if paid work doesn't leave any time for the rest of life, something is very wrong. Catholic social teaching recognizes that while work as we find it is often boring, harmful or even downright dangerous, at its best it can be deeply good for us, even transforming us—and the teaching has a clear vision for how we get there. Work makes so much more sense for me, as I hope it will for you, when we see it through the lens of Catholic social teaching.

The Distinct, Common Worldview behind Catholic Social Teaching

It's important to understand the worldview behind Catholic social teaching because it is not just a set of policy proposals, but a fully formed philosophy about what it means to be human and how humans should care for one another. It's true that you don't have to agree with every aspect of CST's worldview to find it helpful for thinking about work, but I'm going to not-so-subtly suggest that you probably do agree with a lot of it. At least, if you are like my friends from college and the labor movement, mostly secular; or if you're like my students, who range from proudly Catholic to disaffiliated Catholic to proudly Muslim, Jewish, or atheist, I am willing to bet that your view of the meaning of human life and how we should care for each other shares more with Catholic social teaching than the worldview "workism" conveys.

"Workism" is not rooted in an understanding of the human person or how we should care for each other. It values only things that can be counted and given a monetary value, and applies this limited way of valuing to people's lives. In a real way, nonworking adults and all children are not people to modern work culture, because they do not produce outputs that can literally be counted, which are the only results "workism" values. Countable productivity is what matters, even in workplaces like schools and community organizations where turning a profit is not the point. Nobel Prize-winning economist Claudia Goldin describes expectations that professionals be constantly available as "greedy work," meaning that the job itself is greedy for ever more of workers' time and energy.[11] In its assumption that everything that matters can be counted and that more is always better, workism is deeply influenced by US materialism.

Catholic social teaching is not materialist, and it's not only spiritual, either. We call it sacramental or incarnational. Reality is material, what we can see, and also spiritual, things we experience without seeing. (Those who don't believe in God generally find things like love, hope, memories, and moral values to be real, even if we can't see them.) People, too, are both material and spiritual. In Christian theology, *embodiment* refers to the idea that human persons are body-spirit beings, our body as much a part of our selfhood and journey toward God as our souls are. We *are* our bodies; our bodies are parts of our selves, neither disposable containers for the soul nor objects for us to burnish and show off. "In and through embodiment," writes theologian M. Shawn Copeland, "we human persons grasp and realize our essential freedom through engagement and communion with other embodied selves."[12] Freedom, relationship with others, and body-spirit existence are at the core of what it means to be human.

We are our bodies, capable of producing tangible, visible change in the world, and we are our spirits, capable of growing, changing, and transforming in ways that matter deeply even if they are not materially visible. Because our bodies and spirits are linked, it matters what we do with our bodies. How we spend our days affects who we become: "as expressions of our inmost being, our acts have physical, ethical, and spiritual repercussions on ourselves."[13]

I believe that most folks I know, including the brilliant, deeply religion-skeptic folks I've met in higher ed and the labor movement, see the human person as more along Catholic lines than "workism's" materialist perspective. Very few of us, I would argue, actually believe there is no more to reality than what we can observe, or nothing more to value than what can be counted and paid for. We humans think, grow, change, and connect deeply with one another, not just as bodies responding to neurological cues, but as minds and spirits whose transcendent knowing and experience are deeply bound up with—not just carried around by—our physical flesh. If you've ever struggled with a job asking you to do something that goes against your values, or being expected to work at your typical pace while grieving a serious loss, you've encountered the hard truth that "workism" makes little to no room for human nature as both physical and spiritual.

For Catholic social teaching, we have innate human dignity. Because all people are created by God, we all have equal importance and value whether we are wealthy and independent or poor and disabled, incarcerated, unborn, an outsider to the community, powerful, or powerless. "Workism" completely discounts the personhood of those not currently working for pay and thrives on status hierarchies. Many of us have had the experience of a new acquaintance figuring out our professional status and visibly adjusting how warmly or respectfully they treat us. Status inequalities pervade modern work culture at a systemwide level, too. The employed worker can always be threatened with becoming unemployed, the greatest possible loss of status through the "workism" lens, and many workers ignore their own mistreatment as long as there is someone below them in rank to look down on.

Because of our innate human dignity, Catholic social teaching believes we deserve access to our basic needs—food, shelter, clothing, education, etc.—because we are human, not because we work (*Gaudium et Spes* 26). "Workism" prefers to squeeze every drop of productive work out of every human possible, including youth, incarcerated people, and moms who just gave birth, which is why proposals to get people in those groups into (usually low) paying jobs continue to recur in the United States. When we say that only a paid job grants one the right to access basic needs, we're effectively saying that people currently without paid work should starve. Communities have too often been willing to sacrifice unemployed adults and their children to this twisted understanding of human worth, but I believe more and more people are seeing it for the inhumane and frankly ghoulish idea that it is.

Another conviction of Catholic social teaching that I not-so-secretly believe most people share is that as humans, we are not independent, but interdependent. Specifically, we are relational, made up of the relationships that hold and support us; we need others to survive; and we are vulnerable in a way that enables connection with others. Workism envisions the "ideal worker" as without needs, without commitments outside work, without a body that gets sick or injured or needs time to rest, certainly without family dependents.[14] When we need to stop working because we do have all these commitments and need to tend to them, workism treats our needs as an aberration. No actual person—someone with family or friends they care about seeing, who wants to rest on weekends and see their doctor when needed and volunteer in their community and vote in local elections—would design a work system that treats people as so independent they are completely without needs and connections. This, unfortunately, is the work system we have. But it's not the one Catholic social teaching envisions, and this is precisely because the Catholic tradition, like most people I know—again, even the most committed skeptics of religion—knows fully well that humans can't survive without each other.

Throughout the book, I will show how Catholic social teaching's views on work parallel the insights of other thinkers who are scientists, women, community activists, and in other ways very different in their experience and expertise from the popes who have framed Catholic social teaching. For me, this surprising convergence between thinkers from very different periods of history and walks of life is an important reason to pay attention. Another is the fact that Catholic organizations are major employers in the United States, representing thousands of hospitals and healthcare facilities, universities and high schools, and social service organizations. As religion scholars Megan Goodwin and Ilyse Morgenstein Fuerst remind us, "you may be done with religion, but it isn't done with you," particularly if you work for or receive services from a Catholic organization.[15] For those whose lives are affected by Catholic employers, knowing about Catholic teaching on worker justice is an important step toward making sure those organizations live up to the teaching behind their mission.

Catholic social teaching believes that unpaid work is work; that people are more important than property; and that all workers deserve family-supporting wages, good benefits, and the freedom to form a union. These views may produce good results for workers and their families, but the Church's tradition doesn't teach them only for this reason, but because they flow logically from a view of the human person as incarnational, vulnerable, and interdependent. If you share Catholic social teaching's view on any of these specific work policies, it might be because that deeper view of the human person is one you also share.

What Is Catholic Social Teaching?

Even Catholics who go to Mass weekly or who attended Catholic schools or universities are not always familiar with Catholic social teaching. Encyclicals, constitutions of Church councils, and other formal documents that Popes publish to communicate the tradition tend to be long, written in advanced theological language, and not necessarily structured in ways that make their arguments easy to follow. Unlike other important aspects of Catholic belief, like Jesus's resurrection and the Trinity, there are no special days when Catholics around the world will hear sermons on Catholic social teaching. Very few Catholics will ever sit down and read a papal teaching document in its entirety. Those who actively try to learn more about their faith tradition might learn about Catholic social teaching from presentations in their parish, Catholic media, or books like this one. And less involved Catholics or non-Catholics may form their understanding of Catholicism based on secular news media, which tends to focus on headline issues like a new pope or a local scandal, rather than on enduring teachings.

Papal teaching documents are a unique genre, with little in common with other texts we're used to learning from, like magazine articles, political speeches, or online news videos. Some focus on developing a particular concept, like work or protecting the environment, while others address a list of more or less related topics, like "social progress." These documents do not lend themselves well to skimming but do reward repeated reading. (When I am struggling with problems in the world or the Church, I often find comfort in the 1965 constitution *Gaudium et Spes*, where the Church's bishops turned a loving gaze on aspects of the real world, from politics to families to the arts. I try to reread it about once a year.) Sometimes papal teaching documents recommend particular solutions to problems, but sometimes they simply mention the problem's existence as a way to signal that the Church knows it exists and needs to be addressed. Examples include discrimination against women, inequalities following colonization, or climate change, each of which Catholic social teaching acknowledged as serious problems at times in history when many denied their existence or wrote them off as "just the way things are."

A pope issues an encyclical when he wants to say something from his position at the highest level of the Church's authority, to convey that not just he as an individual, but the Church and its historical tradition are speaking. Popes have a privileged role in interpreting the Catholic tradition and, as global leaders, have a wealth of information on human experience available to them if they ask, but that does not mean that every word out of a Pope's mouth is an infallible statement of Church authority. Catholics understand that we can distinguish between what a Pope might say in an interview, a sermon, or even a book that reflects his own viewpoint, and what he teaches in an encyclical over his signature, which is an authoritative teaching of the Church tradition in continuity with the understanding of previous generations. Documents from Vatican Council II, like *Gaudium et Spes*, are issued over the signature of a Pope but technically carry an even greater level of authority, because a council of all the world's bishops approved those teachings together. The *Compendium of the Social Doctrine of the Church* is another authoritative document I cite in this book; it is essentially a lengthy summary of the Catholic social teaching documents before 2004.

For the most part, and in all the teaching this book will cover, Popes see themselves as advancing a consistent tradition rather than changing earlier Church teachings or promoting their own agendas. Scholars might debate the distinctions between popes or the influences on their ideas, but this book will reflect Catholic social teaching's self-understanding that the tradition is the same truth throughout time, although it may be presented in a new way appropriate to changing realities. Similarly, some scholars distinguish between Catholic social *teaching*, the encyclicals and other authoritative statements from the Church hierarchy, and Catholic social *thought*, the broader tradition of responses to that teaching by those outside Church leadership. For the purposes of this book, that distinction is not important.[16] I am focusing on authoritative statements by Popes, because when generations of world leaders use the power of religious authority to argue that governments should support workers by limiting the power of business owners, every worker (and owner) owes it to themselves to pay attention. I do refer to the work of scholars and others outside the Church hierarchy to help us understand the points being made by the authoritative tradition.

Catholic social teaching on work draws from two primary theological sources: natural law and the Bible. When John Paul II discusses Jesus as a worker, for example, he is referencing the Bible, which Catholics understand to be God's revelation of the divine plan. We can also understand God's plan by observing human nature as we find it around us: this source of insight into God's design is called the natural law. While not everyone believes that the Bible reveals God's plan, drawing moral insights from human nature is something anyone, of any faith, can do (in fact, something nearly all of us do without thinking about it). A technical way of putting this is to say that natural law is intelligible to anyone by the light of reason, not by the light of faith. When I worked at a labor union, some of my colleagues had had bad personal experiences with the Catholic Church or Catholic employers, but they respected Catholic social teaching's view of worker dignity, which was a source of common ground. One doesn't need to accept the teaching authority of the Catholic Church to see internal logic in its social teaching, which comes from the natural law that everybody can access through reason.

Neither natural law arguments nor biblical arguments are necessarily "progressive" or "conservative" in the way we tend to classify political beliefs in the United States. Welcoming refugees or migrants without conditions is a position with strong Biblical roots. When someone uses the happiness and stability of same-sex relationships they know in order to argue for legal protection for same-sex marriage, they are making a natural law argument, saying that such relationships can be good for human beings and for society. Many of Catholic social teaching's views on worker justice and the economy would be considered politically progressive in the United States, to the left of the national Democratic Party. But the Church does not hold these views for any political reason; rather, they flow naturally from Catholic beliefs about the human person.

Catholics traditionally refer to encyclicals by their Latin titles, which are the first few words of the document and don't necessarily reveal much about its content. For example, *Quadragesimo Anno* (1931) is about work and economic inequality, but its Latin title literally means "In the fortieth year." Encyclicals have formal English titles that reveal more about their topic—*Quadragesimo Anno*'s is "On Reconstruction of the Social Order"—but are not as widely used. In this book, I will stick with the Latin titles for consistency and because, as I said above, this book is less interested in differences between the encyclicals than in the message of the tradition as a whole.

For most of Catholic social teaching's history, the original versions of encyclicals were published in Latin, and the Vatican distributed official translations into other languages, including English, for anyone to publish for free. These days, official translations are shared on the Vatican website, with versions in many languages often appearing simultaneously. Official translations are not updated once they are made, so older ones reflect the English used in earlier decades and centuries. The most noticeably dated result is that English translations of older encyclicals use "men" to refer to all people. Since my goal in this book is to show how Catholic social teaching applies to all workers—whether they work for pay or in the home, and of any gender—I have paraphrased official Church documents, used publicly available inclusive-language translations, or done my own translations from the Latin in instances where "man" is used in a way that would confuse a modern reader, or where the older style of English used is simply unclear.

For Catholics, papal teaching documents are authoritative statements of Church teaching, not conveying God's word directly in the same way as the Bible, but an important part of our tradition that we should attempt to understand and take seriously. But encyclicals have always been intended to reach non-Catholics as well, which mass media and now the Internet have helped them do. When Pope Francis released *Laudato Si'*, his long-anticipated encyclical on care for the environment, in 2015, it was fascinating to watch my inbox fill up with responses from secular "green" nonprofits applauding the insights and goals of this Catholic teaching document. You do not have to be Catholic, or agree with everything the Catholic Church teaches or does, to benefit from learning more about Catholic social teaching. If you're concerned about making a better work life for yourself or for others, I believe this tradition can help you think about how we get there.

What to Expect

This introduction has proposed that aspects of the way we commonly think about work today are harmful, including "workism," the idea that work for pay is the source of personal dignity, identity, and worth, and the "labor-of-love myth," the idea that loving our paid work is the path to happiness. Catholic social teaching, a body of insights on the human person and economic life created by Catholic bishops and popes, presents a better way of thinking about the nature of work and its purpose in a well-lived human life. Catholic social teaching is rooted in an understanding of the human person that I propose most people of any or no faith share, one that sees all people as possessed of equal dignity and worth; made up of body, mind, and spirit; and interdependent, meaning we need to rely on one another in order to survive and thrive. Finally, I explained the ways Catholic social teaching is created and shared, noting that popes and bishops who frame Catholic social teaching regard it as one internally consistent tradition, even though it may be expressed in different ways to respond to changing realities.

Chapter 2 will explain Catholic social teaching's inclusive definition of work. Different from the common understanding that work is what we do for pay, work in Catholic social teaching is any activity where humans use our abilities to transform any aspect of the world around us. It is work whether the activity is paid or unpaid, and whether it helps us develop our skills and talents or alienates us from our true human nature. This chapter will explain why the various aspects of this inclusive definition help us value the contributions of all workers and understand certain problems with work as we find it in the world today.

Unpaid care within the family, the topic of Chapter 3, consists of important tasks that can take up all of an adult's waking hours, but which some still describe as "not working." Applying CST's inclusive definition of work helps us see unpaid care for the challenging, skilled labor that it is, and helps us understand two of the tradition's convictions about unpaid care work: that it is work, equal in dignity and importance with paid work, and that since care is important to the well-being and future of communities, this work deserves financial compensation from the community. Catholic social teaching finds common ground here with the work of economists, sociologists, and other experts who study care outside theology.

We often think of work as something that depletes and exhausts us, but at other times we find that involving ourselves in a challenging task—something Catholic social teaching would consider work—can restore our energy and spirits. Chapter 4 examines this paradoxical quality of work through the work of food preparation. Scientists tell us that involvement in physical labor can help us "complete the stress cycle," and philosophers suggest that manual labor calls upon our gifts of attention and pragmatism when we respond to the real qualities of something that exists outside ourselves. For all these reasons, food preparation work can be good for us even though it may be extra work added on top of a paid job. Catholic social teaching also singles out farm work's importance to entire communities that depend on food—so much so that the single case where the tradition calls on government to seize private property has to do with unjust hoarding of farmland. For historical reasons, work growing and preparing food is often some of the most dangerous and poorly paid of any paid work, but understanding Catholic social teaching's concept of the "indirect employer" helps envision a path to more justice for the workers who feed us.

While work is good for us, the Catholic tradition also insists that human beings need intentional experiences of nonproductivity, which the philosopher Josef Pieper called leisure. As Chapter 5 shows, Pieper's thought on leisure is strikingly similar to contemporary works by artist-thinkers who advocate practices of rest and attention as resistance to the contemporary overvaluing of productivity. All believe that deliberate inactivity is crucial for the well-being of humans and their communities. This view is echoed by working artists whom I interviewed in a quest to better understand whether artmaking is work or leisure. These artists' insights point to the conclusion that artmaking itself is work, but that intentional downtime is important, not only for creative workers like artists, but for every human worker. Securing access to downtime for every worker will require better structures—both changing our own attitudes about productivity and worth, and creating social support for nonwork time, such as universal basic income. Practicing leisure, which celebrates the goodness of what is, can help inspire us in solidarity to build communities where every worker can enjoy restorative times of nonproductivity.

Chapter 6 examines the wages and working conditions that make paid work just, worthy of human dignity. Unsafe conditions and unjust wages are sadly widespread today. Catholic social teaching understands that the indirect employer—those large powers, such as governments, that shape the economic conditions in which work takes place—shares responsibility for wages and working conditions with direct employers. Economic coercion is one reason why many people are working full time and still not making ends meet, something Catholic social teaching regards as deeply wrong. Just compensation for paid work means wages that can support a worker and their family, which can take the form of a family wage, family grants, or universal basic income, all proposals supported in Catholic social teaching documents. Just compensation also includes retirement security, health care, and regular time away from work.

The final chapter asks what we can do—as workers, employers, and together as a society—to make work work for us. Governments have a significant role in defending workers' rights due to the power imbalance between workers and employers, although many employers today also realize that paying living wages is good business. Finally, workers have the power to win just wages and safe working conditions when they form unions with other workers. Catholic social teaching's views on just wages and working conditions and how workers can attain them stem from the tradition's understanding of the human person as vulnerable, relational, and transcendent. We can understand work better and bring our paid and unpaid work into better harmony when we operate using Catholic social teaching's inclusive definition of work: work is all the things we do in the process of making a life.

Notes

1 Daniel Schneider and Kristen Harknett, "Consequences of Routine Work-Schedule Instability for Worker Health and Well-Being," *American Sociological Review* 84, no. 1 (February 1, 2019): 82, https://doi.org/10.1177/0003122418823184.

2 Derek Thompson, "Workism Is Making Americans Miserable," *The Atlantic*, February 24, 2019, https://www.theatlantic.com/ideas/archive/2019/02/religion-workism-making-americans-miserable/583441/.
3 Jonathan Malesic, *The End of Burnout: Why Work Drains Us and How to Build Better Lives* (Oakland: University of California Press, 2022), 3.
4 Malesic, *The End of Burnout*, 3.
5 Sarah Jaffe, *Work Won't Love You Back: How Devotion to Our Jobs Keeps Us Exploited, Exhausted, and Alone* (New York: Bold Type Books, 2021), 322.
6 Anne Helen Petersen, *Can't Even: How Millennials Became the Burnout Generation* (Boston: Mariner Books, 2020), 69.
7 Jaffe, *Work Won't Love You Back*, 9.
8 This view has been held by Christians long before Catholic social teaching, being strongly asserted in the Hebrew Bible, which Christians hold as authoritative Scripture. Thanks to my colleague Matthew Neujahr for many generative conversations around the provision of basic needs in the Hebrew Bible.
9 Samhita Mukhopadhyay, *The Myth of Making It: A Workplace Reckoning* (New York: Random House, 2024), 84–6; Cal Newport, "The Year in Quiet Quitting," *The New Yorker*, December 29, 2022, https://www.newyorker.com/culture/2022-in-review/the-year-in-quiet-quitting.
10 Francis, "To Managers and Delegates of the Italian General Confederation of Labor (CGIL)," *Vatican.va*, December 19, 2022, https://www.vatican.va/content/francesco/en/speeches/2022/december/documents/20221219-cgil.html.
11 Claudia Dale Goldin, *Career and Family: Women's Century-Long Journey toward Equity*, Ebook Collection (JSTOR) (Princeton, NJ: Princeton University Press, 2021), 10.
12 M. Shawn Copeland, *Enfleshing Freedom: Body, Race, and Being* (Minneapolis, MN: Fortress Press, 2010), 8.
13 Ferdinand Tablan, "Catholic Social Teachings: Toward a Meaningful Work," *Journal of Business Ethics* 128, no. 2 (2015): 295.
14 Christine Firer Hinze, *Glass Ceilings and Dirt Floors: Women, Work, and the Global Economy*, 2014 Madeleva Lecture in Spirituality (Mahwah, NJ: Paulist Press, 2015), 82.
15 Megan Goodwin and Elyse Morgenstein Fuerst, "Episode 106: You May Be Done with Religion, but Religion Isn't Done with You," Keeping It 101: A Killjoy's Introduction to Religion Podcast, accessed January 14, 2025, https://keepingit101.com/e106.
16 For some Catholics, it's really important to know which ideas come from Church authority and which do not. Other readers, including

many Catholics, will be equally open to ideas that do not come from, or may even disagree with, Church authority. People in both groups frequently have thoughtful, hard-won reasons for their relationships with authoritative teaching, and I respect both viewpoints. My own understanding of Church history indicates that there have been times throughout history when arguments disagreeing with the position then held by Church authority have been important for helping Catholics better understand and teach God's plan for the Church. Some perceive the result as changed teaching and others as improved articulation of a consistently held position. (See John Noonan, Jr., *A Church That Can and Cannot Change: The Development of Catholic Moral Teaching* (Notre Dame, IN: University of Notre Dame Press, 2005.) I focus on the authoritative teaching documents in this book because, as I said above, the papal teaching on work and worker dignity is one that every worker, of any or no faith, deserves to know and to take seriously.

2

Making a Life: Work and Human Purpose

Chapter Outline

Work: It's Not What You Think	20
Work and Human Purpose	21
Work Is Good for Us	26
Work as a Duty	28
If Work Is Good for Us, Why Is It Often So Bad?	31
Is There Life Beyond Work?	36
Conclusion	38

This chapter explains the nuances of Catholic social teaching's inclusive definition of work and points to how we see work differently when we understand it as more than what we do for pay. Catholic social teaching (CST) understands that humans have a deep, innate desire to innovate and create, collaborate with others, and change ourselves and the world around us, and the tradition views all these types of purposeful activity as work. This means work is much more than a paid job, but a uniquely human way of existing in the world, shaping it and ourselves. Because work is a human activity, its primary importance is how it shapes the worker, rather than what the work produces.

Work is a duty for humans, but that doesn't mean every adult should work for pay—indeed, everyone deserves times of life that are protected from paid work. Two things are true at the same time: while work, in the broad sense, is important to a meaningful life, human dignity precedes, and does not depend on, productivity. Any attempt to *equate* work with human worth, or to make paid employment compulsory, goes against the view of Catholic social teaching: work is "an integral part of the human condition, although not the only purpose of life" (*Compendium* 264).

Finally, work in general is good for us, but work as we find it in the real world can be deeply harmful. When something is wrong with work, something is wrong in our lives. When people who want work can't find it; when work is harmful, degrading, or underpaid; or when workers are kept from joining together to improve their working conditions, they are missing out on what they need, and deserve, for a fully human life. It's important to understand what work is and what good work looks like to fight toward the goal of good work for all.

Work: It's Not What You Think

For Catholic social teaching, work is any activity through which humans transform the world—any of the things, systems, and people around us—using our uniquely human abilities to create, reason, and learn. Paid employment is obviously work, but so are many things that are not typically done for pay. If it would be work if you paid someone to do it, it's work when you do it for yourself, including cooking, yard work, making appointments, dealing with your budget, and all the other tasks that are part of taking care of yourself, your home and possessions, your loved ones, and your community.

The tradition often describes work as transforming "creation," or the material of the world around us; in work we shape God's creation to make it more useful to humans. This way of describing work references the Biblical story of the Garden of Eden, where God gave Adam and Eve the responsibility to "cultivate and care for" the earth (Genesis 2, NAB; *LE* 9). We might imagine transforming creation as looking like farming or manufacturing; it's obvious how those work activities transform the created material of the world. But humans are God's creation too, of course—so nurses, teachers, and therapists transform creation as they shape the lives of their students or patients. We transform ourselves, and we work, when we learn or exercise. Finally, when we apply our creative agency to bring things into being, whether literature and art, tax returns and spreadsheets, policies and laws, or our own social media presence, we are working.

It's common to think of "work" as tasks done for pay at a workplace, and unpaid labor as simply a part of life—so much so that a parent putting in sixteen-hour days to care for their own kids is treated by economists, and may be dismissed by peers, as "not working." But Catholic social teaching has always recognized unpaid work as work, equal in dignity and importance with the work we do for pay. The first document of modern Catholic social teaching, Leo XIII's *Rerum Novarum*, talked about women's "work" in the home in 1891. Ninety years later, John Paul II included caring for children and the home in a list of work that can be difficult "toil," even though it is very important (*LE* 9). In books about Catholic social teaching, it is common to acknowledge that the tradition counts unpaid work as work, and then continue as if this were not the case, writing about "work" using examples from, or discussing issues with, paid employment only. This book will not make that mistake. Looking at work in its fullness—paid and unpaid, in the workplace, home, artist's studio, volunteer setting, social media platform, and everywhere work is done—is crucial to understanding what it means for us and how to draw forth the meaning work can have for our lives.

Work and Human Purpose

Work is important for how it changes the world, but more so for how it changes the worker.

This is another radical insight of Catholic social teaching that is profoundly countercultural to the way we often think of work. If work transforms us in harmful ways—breaking down our bodies, making us cynical or depressed—most of us have learned to see that as the cost of having a job. People who find themselves struggling with the way a job is changing them might be shut down with the rejoinder, "That's why they call it work." Should we expect our work to improve us as people, helping us develop skills and grow? We might see that as an aspirational goal, even a luxury. But for Catholic social teaching, the most important aspect of work, the key to evaluating it morally, is how work changes the worker.

To delve further into this, we need some technical vocabulary. The terms can be confusing, and I would have chosen different ones myself, but well—that's why they call it work.

Work is important for how it changes the world, but more so for how it changes the worker. In the jargon of Catholic social teaching, we'd say, "Work is important for its objective dimension, but more so for its subjective dimension," or "The subjective sense of work takes priority over its objective sense." The results work produces—the goods manufactured, the systems improved, the students educated, or the patients healed—are the work's objective dimension. The subjective sense of work refers to how doing the work shapes the worker. (In English, "dimension" and "sense" are used interchangeably to name these two aspects of work.)

Sometimes we use the words "subjective" and "objective" to describe ideas or arguments. When one of my students calls an idea "subjective," she's usually saying that it seems to be based on the thinker's own perspective, rather than observable fact; perhaps it is true in different ways for different people. But that isn't how John Paul II, who introduced work's subjective and objective dimensions in *Laborem Exercens*, is using the words. In Catholic thought, "subjective" looks at work through its impact on the worker who does it, who is the *subject* of work. The things we work on, the *objects* of our labor, are what we're thinking about with work's objective sense. Work in its objective sense looks at what's being done and what results. We might think of work in its objective sense as work-as-doing, and work in its subjective sense as work-as-becoming. Or, we could look at work in its objective sense as what we make (understanding that we make changes as well as things), and work in its subjective sense as what work makes us into.

By pointing to humans as the *subject* of work, John Paul II is not saying that work rules over us like a king does his subjects; he is highlighting the human's role as the animator, the doer, of work. In grammar, the *subject* of a sentence is the one doing the action the sentence describes. In Catholic thought, work, a human activity, is always done *by someone*. So, for example, the subject of mining is a miner; the objective results produced are valuable minerals; and the subjective sense of work appears in the way work shapes the miner when she develops strong muscles or lung disease. The subject of writing is a writer; the objective results (let's say) are a book;

and the long hours spent at a desk may make the writer more reflective or more antisocial. The subject of caregiving is a caregiver; the objective results produced are the ongoing well-being of a child or vulnerable adult; and the subjective sense of work may find the caregiver becoming more tuned in to others' needs and perhaps less attentive to his own. Mining, writing, and care do not exist in some general abstract form; they are human tasks, done by humans working.

Maybe you think it's obvious that work is done by human beings, and you naturally picture the writers when you watch a favorite TV show or the miners when you hear about a semiconductor shortage. But think about how terms like "productivity," "imports," "content," or "employment" are used to describe the results of human work without ever mentioning a human worker. The priority importance of work's subjective sense in Catholic social teaching reminds us to hear "productivity is up" and think "humans are producing more goods and services in the same amount of time," or hear "unemployment increase" and think "more people who want work can't access it." Realizing that work is done by human workers is key to getting our economic and ethical understandings of work right.

Work is a human activity. It involves not just completing tasks, but also reasoned, contextual decision-making about the tasks. Because only a human being is "a conscious and free subject, . . . a subject that decides about [them]self," only human beings work (*LE* 6). Our language often suggests that animals or machines work—think about the way "mixing" or "printing" describe specific human behaviors, even though we often use machines to do them. But unlike an animal or machine, a human decides when to start and stop their task and uses reasoning to incorporate their previous experience of the task into the way they do it today. Think about the way a skilled restaurant server knows which tables want attention and which want privacy; surgeons or builders direct their hands with intuitive precision; or a caregiver knows how to pull a child back from the brink of a tantrum. These kinds of knowledge are crucial to doing work well, and can't fully be taught because they are not entirely known through reason or articulable in language. Placing a scalpel just where it needs to go or using the right tone of voice to calm a fussy baby or frustrated customer are tasks of the body as much as they are of the mind—or better, they are tasks of the human person, who is body, mind, and spirit. Humans are embodied spirits, inspirited beings; our bodies are part of who we are, not simply meat carriers for our brains. Machines can help complete tasks, but work takes place when we use our reason to transform the goods of creation. Only humans complete the reason-based transformation of the goods of creation that Catholic social teaching considers "work."

When John Paul II laid out the distinctions between work's objective and subjective dimensions in *Laborem Exercens* (1981), he wrote during a time of the greatest economic prosperity in many countries' history. Certainly, backbreaking, unsafe labor was all too common in many places, as it is today. But during John Paul II's papacy, many workers in wealthier countries had improved their standard of living enough to expect more from their work. With twentieth-century advancements in workplace safety, workers in many parts of the globe now had the relative privilege to ask whether their work reflected their deep yearnings and desires as individuals. (Think about the ways literature and music of the 1960s and 1970s presented office work as stifling individuality, when a few generations earlier saw safe, clean office work as a luxury compared to manual labor.[1]) Workers struggling to survive rarely pause to ask whether they are fulfilled, but in the new prosperity of the twentieth century, many workers could expect fulfillment, vocation, and purpose from their work. In this climate of searching for meaning, *Laborem Exercens* was right on time.

John Paul II was not the first thinker to point our attention to how work affects the worker. In 1776, the economic philosopher Adam Smith memorably, if tactlessly, observed that repetitive manufacturing work made workers "as stupid and ignorant as it is possible for a human creature to become."[2] When women took jobs in Industrial Revolution factories, commentators worried their bodies would break under the hard work and their morals would suffer from being around men outside their families.[3] When John Paul II named the distinction between work's product (objective sense) and its impact on the worker (subjective sense), he gave a crucial refocus to the twentieth century's pride in productivity by insisting that the subjective sense mattered *more* than the objective sense. Work's impact on the worker matters *more* than the minerals mined, the books written, the profits produced, or any other quantifiable result of work. Products are property, but workers are people; and people, in Catholic thinking, always matter more than property. How work affects the worker is more important than the goods the work produces.

In my class on Catholic social teaching on work, I asked for examples of work that our mainstream culture values more for its subjective element than its objective results. I thought it might be a tough question, but a student's hand shot right up: "It's us!" Exactly! Education is an example of work that even our results-obsessed culture intuitively values for its subjective sense. Students expend reasoned, embodied, intentional effort to transform the goods of creation—themselves—to develop their innate abilities, reliably access some of the vast store of human knowledge, and prepare to contribute in their own fields. Most people understand that the paper a student writes or the tests she takes create value for that student and her community, even though no one is paying her.

If we can appreciate work for its subjective element when we observe how we grow and improve through performing our work tasks, we can also notice the ways work's subjective element can interfere with our flourishing as human beings. Distinguishing between work's objective and subjective senses gives us an accurate language for the ways work can harm us.

The subjective sense of work includes elements that are inherent to the nature of the work as well as conditions that are not inherent to the work, which could be changed to improve the subjective impact on the worker. For example, some jobs will always be more dangerous than office work, but professions like logging and mining are safer for workers today than they were hundreds of years ago because workers in those fields understood that some dangers were not inherent to their work and fought for better safety protections. Work in a shipping fulfillment center may have an unavoidable element of boring monotony, but whether it is also unbearably stressful and pain-inducing might depend on how many items workers are expected to handle per hour, the length of their breaks, and the design of their workspaces—working conditions that are not inherent to the tasks. We can think of many examples where the same work might provide an exciting challenge to some, while leaving others without opportunities to exercise their skills and talents. The subjects of work, human beings, are all different, and the way work shapes them will depend on their unique individuality. Even when work's inherent nature would tend to make it beneficial in terms of the subjective sense, working conditions can override it. For example, health care providers may develop increased empathy through their work with patients, but employer demands to treat many patients in a short time can lead to burnout, generating cynicism, not empathy, toward the people a worker serves.[4]

Work Is Good for Us

Work is good for us. This is because of work's subjective and objective senses. It is good for us because through work (paid or unpaid) we provide for our own needs and those of others, and we develop our own abilities, as we'll talk about more in the following chapter. Although work in certain cases can be harmful, work in general is a good thing for humans. Some Christians historically viewed work as God's punishment for sin, but Catholic social teaching rejects that view. Work is so central to our human nature that it would have been part of life even if we were not sinners, according to Leo XIII: if humans had not fallen from the "state of innocence" through sin, we would still work, but through "free will and for our souls' delight," instead of out of necessity (*RN* 17). The story of Adam and Eve, which Leo references here, indicates that God created humans good, but sin is part of our lives as a result of the free choice which God also gave us. Work in general, in its essence, is part of our nature and good for us. Although work as we often find it can be harmful and even degrading, Leo XIII suggests that these realities are the result of sin, not part of the nature of work.

As an example, making useful objects seems to be part of our human nature. Even very young children quickly develop the insight to climb on one thing to reach another, or the imagination to turn a stick into a wand or baseball bat. The abuses Leo XIII observed in Industrial Revolution factories are not inherent to the human task of making objects, which is a good and useful part of many flourishing lives. Exploitative work is the result of sin—of the greed of factory owners who demanded long hours and dangerous practices, or of the callousness of adults who tolerated the practice of child labor. Similarly, we could imagine a worker in a modern weapons factory who works in clean, ergonomic comfort but is tormented with guilt at the violence her work enables. Here again, Leo XIII would not deny that this work is harmful and would probably advise the worker to find other employment, but still, the harm is not due to the fact that she is working. A job may be safe and secure for human bodies while harming the part of us that is spiritual and connected to others, as when our work enables the violent destruction of other human lives.

Work is so good for us that it is one way we live out our relationship with God. Through our work, paid or unpaid, we serve God by serving one another. It is even accurate to say that our paid or unpaid work is something God has called us to because people need one another to provide food, heal the sick, raise the next generation, and do all the other tasks that allow us to live together in society. This understanding—that ordinary work is a way for people to serve God—is part of modern Catholic social teaching and has its roots in the practice of early Catholic religious communities, but it is strongly associated with the teaching of the reformer Martin Luther (1483–1546.) Luther hoped to reform the Catholic Church from what he saw as its errors, one of which was teaching that only priests or nuns had a vocation or "calling" from God to lead holy lives. Rather, Luther taught—as the Catholic Church now teaches—that every Christian is called to pursue holiness in the course of their ordinary tasks. Work is important, and everyone can pursue a spiritual life by serving others, even if we are doing so through our ordinary paid or unpaid work.

People who feel a strong connection of personal values to their paid or unpaid work will often refer to it as their vocation. The Catholic tradition teaches that vocation is strongly linked to the work we do, even though a vocation is not reducible to any particular job. Vatican Council II envisioned a person's "total vocation" as becoming who they are uniquely created and called to be, with work a key way we learn about ourselves and develop our gifts. "When [humans] work, not only do they transform matter and society, they also perfect themselves. They learn, develop their faculties, emerging from and transcending themselves. . . . Here then is the norm for human activity: to harmonize with the authentic interests of the human race, in accordance with God's will and design, and to enable people as individuals and as members of society to pursue and fulfill their total vocation" (*GS* 35).[5] Work is important to realizing our vocation, which is to shape ourselves into who we are called to be, and the habitual, repeated tasks of work are an important way we shape ourselves. But this is different from saying that who we are called to be is a doctor, parent, writer, or any other type of worker. Many people do feel that God has called them to a specific work role, but Catholic social teaching does not see every person's vocation as a specific job, but as becoming who God created them to be.

In the young adult novel *Catherine, Called Birdy*, a wise woman tells the young protagonist, "In the world to come, you will not be asked 'Why were you not George?' or 'Why were you not Perkin?,'" naming other characters in the story, "but 'Why were you not Catherine?'"[6] Catherine, a young woman in medieval England, goes on to realize that whatever path her future takes, "I will still be me."[7] To help my students reflect on their vocation as distinct from a paid job, I ask them to imagine how they might continue to live out their vocation if the career they envision were no longer possible—for example, because of health problems or the need to relocate. Our work, paid and unpaid, is an important part of who we are, but not the whole of who we are called to be. Even less does any particular paid job describe the whole of God's call for each of us.

Work as a Duty

Because work is good for us and an important way we contribute to the world, Catholic social teaching talks about it as a duty, something every human should do. This teaching is often misunderstood, so it's crucial to remember the inclusive definition of work as being both paid and unpaid when we think about work as a duty.

We must work in order to fulfill God's will for our lives, to develop our skills and potential, and to help our families, our societies, and future generations of humanity (*LE* 16). Other people need the results of our labor, our work's objective dimension, to survive and flourish, just as we need theirs. Especially in the United States, with our famously excessive work culture and comparatively meager welfare state, Catholic scholars have tended to interpret the duty to work by suggesting that adults have the duty to work *for pay* if they are able to do so.[8] This does tend to be the way mainstream US culture looks at work—that a paid job is the duty of every capable adult—but it is a distortion of Catholic teaching.

If US interpreters of Catholic social teaching tend to present the duty to work as a duty to paid work, one reason may be that the most common example, in papal documents, of unpaid work is (what is presented as) women's work in the home.[9] Mainstream US culture has not traditionally viewed the work of homemakers and caregivers as "work," and perhaps US interpreters fall prey to this cultural stigma when they drift into depicting the duty to work as a duty to paid labor.[10] This is unfortunate, because the papal tradition's discussion of women's work—although it is limited by the gendered views of its authors and their times—holds profound insights for correctly understanding the duty to work as it applies to every person, and for the public policies that rest on our assumptions about work and human dignity.

Since Catholic social teaching insists that unpaid work is work, the obvious conclusion is that any productive, creative human activity fulfills the duty to work. The tradition discusses the "work" of artists, entrepreneurs, community volunteers, and family caregivers, people whose labor clearly uses human abilities to transform creation, even as it is rarely paid. The downside of inadvertently implying that every adult has a duty to hold a paid job is devaluing the important unpaid work that supports families, communities, and cultures, implying that adults who contribute in those important ways are falling short. In fact, one papal encyclical even specifies that people who are able to live without paid labor deserve to be allowed to do so (*QA* 57). In historical context, I believe this refers to people of independent wealth, who are the most likely in any community to be able to live without a paid job. But it's interesting to note that most of us don't worry much about whether the independently wealthy are spending their time in productive pursuits. The duty to work does not insist that every adult must be in the paid workforce, but that every adult should spend their energies transforming creation in order to be of use to themselves and others. Family caregivers are absolutely fulfilling that duty, and urging them into the paid workforce is a misunderstanding of the teaching.

Understanding family care as fulfilling the duty to work reminds us of CST's consistent teaching that people have the right to waged work that suits their abilities, needs, and family situations. This message has been framed in a variety of ways, some of which are widely accepted today and others which we might find problematic. For example, *Rerum Novarum*, in 1881, wrote that "work which is quite suitable for a strong man cannot rightly be required from a woman or a child" and warned that children should not work "in workshops and factories until their bodies and minds are sufficiently developed" (42). When we remember that child labor was not outlawed in the United States until the Fair Labor Standards Act of 1937 (and is still legal on farms), we can see that Leo XIII was progressive indeed in telling the industrial capitalism of his time that just because a person *can* produce wealth for their employers under certain conditions does not mean it is right for them to do so. At the same time, we would not regard it as progressive today to group women and children together as those in need of special exclusion from, or protection within, the labor market.

As a woman, I bristle at Leo XIII assuming all women are equally incapable of difficult physical labor, but I can also see how even well into the twenty-first century, our economies have a long way to go toward achieving his goal of working conditions that account for workers' physical and relational needs. Throughout the twentieth century, women sought to win respect and economic freedom by showing they could do the same work as men did, under the same conditions. They have done so amazingly, so that it becomes much harder to say with Leo XIII that there are things men can do that women can't. Today, women excel in the military, construction, athletics, and other "strong-man" working roles that would astonish the author of *Rerum Novarum*.[11] However, the other side of the coin that Leo recognized—that work should accommodate the needs of the worker—has been left behind by women's stellar success in adapting to a working world designed for men. We have gone from assuming that a man could be an "ideal worker," always available, because his wife at home took care of the house and kids, to expecting workers of all genders to be such "ideal workers," with no social provisions made for child care.[12] Work in many professions remains designed for an average male body, meaning everything from no time off for childbearing in medical residencies to poorly designed protective gear that exposes women to on-the-job injury and death.[13]

It is easy to hear the way Leo XIII and other framers of CST talk about women as patriarchal, and I am not about to try to convince you that a Pope is anything other than a patriarch! However, two things can be true at once: the language of papal statements does not always honor women in the way feminists today rightly expect, *and* their overall message—work should accommodate the worker's embodied needs, not the other way around—remains, even today, a radically progressive dream. The aging worker, the pregnant worker, and the worker with disabilities continue to be regarded as anomalous, a liability, in too many workplace contexts, despite how stunningly common such conditions are to the human experience. Perhaps we can overlook dated phrasing when the message it carries is one our society is still failing to hear.

Fully living into CST's understanding that work is both paid and unpaid could result in profound changes: more respect for unpaid work and the workers who do it, even the public will to support their work with an income. At the same time, all humans have a responsibility to do what they must to preserve their own lives, and for many, that will mean earning a living through work (*CA* 8). The duty to work places responsibilities on communities to create the conditions for people to fulfill it, another important reason many interpreters focus on paid work when they talk about this duty. If we have a duty to preserve our lives, and if work is the most common way to survive in a given society, communities must ensure that those who need to do so can access work at wages that will support them. (We will talk more about community support for people not currently working for pay in Chapter 6.) Catholic teaching insists that there is a duty to work, not because the tradition imagines that people will sit down and starve unless we remind them of their duty, but to highlight the fact that where there is a duty that springs from human nature, there is a right to be able to fulfill that duty, and a responsibility for communities to make that possible.

If Work Is Good for Us, Why Is It Often So Bad?

The duty to work does not mean that everyone has a duty to work for pay, and it definitely does not mean that paid workers should accept any job they can find, no matter how unjust the wages and conditions. Catholic social teaching insists that wages and conditions for paid work should honor workers' human dignity and need for relational connection and rest. Work should allow us to develop our creative capabilities and support a family on one worker's wages. It is obvious that many, perhaps most, working situations today do not live up to this high ideal, from well-paid jobs that place unreasonable demands on time, to jobs that pay poverty wages, to the extreme injustices of incarcerated labor and modern slavery. Catholic social teaching's understanding of work holds out a highly aspirational view of what work should be, while remaining fully realistic about work as we too often encounter it in the world.

Even though Catholic social teaching holds out an idealistic vision of what work can be at its best, it still regards work that is bad, monotonous, or even grossly exploitative as *work*. This might seem like a petty distinction, but it matters for how we think about work in our lives and our communities. We might be tempted to say that since work is a human activity, only those activities and conditions that are worthy of human dignity should be considered work. For example, the philosopher Ferdinand Tablan insists that "any human activity that violates human dignity and treats the human person simply as a tool of production cannot be considered work," suggesting that a significant portion of work as we find it in the real world should be considered something else.[14] Tablan is trying to stress how important it is to Catholic social teaching that work *should* treat people as persons and respect their human dignity. But he misses an important nuance: requiring work to be good in order to be work defines work in such a way that only the most personally fulfilling jobs done under the most dignified and comfortable conditions could possibly qualify. As we've seen, Catholic social teaching sees work as everything that humans do to shape the world around them. We could subdivide this larger category into work that is good (dignified and human) and "bad work." Bad work could include work performed under unjust conditions that would otherwise be dignified and human, and a distinct category of work that is dehumanizing in ways that are intrinsic to the work's nature, which CST calls "alienating work."

Catholic social teaching describes work as "alienating" when it literally separates us, alienates us, from our own human nature, which the tradition describes according to several key features. Humans are *creative*, able to use our powers of reason and forethought to solve problems in a way that is unique to us and reminds us of God's own creativity. We are *vulnerable*. Our bodies age and break down; need food, rest, and human contact; and remind us that we are not machines. We are *capable of transcendence*. In these vulnerable earthly bodies coexists a spirit capable of great dreams, heroic generosity, and the desire for joy, insight, and connection through which we seek God. And our vulnerability and capacity for transcendence make us *relational*, seeking out community with other humans and with God. These relationships, in turn, shape and make up who we are.

When we think about our human nature as being creative, vulnerable, transcendent, and relational, we can see how work could interfere with fully living into our nature's potential. Monotonous work, performed under conditions of high control where we have little input into daily tasks, could, over time, alienate us from our creative nature. (When the Catholic social teaching documents talk about alienating work, they often seem to have in mind the repetitious tasks of nineteenth-century manufacturing.[15]) Some work treats humans as disposable machine components, failing to respect our vulnerable nature; think about the superhuman effort glorified in the John Henry legend, or the digital surveillance tools that push Amazon warehouse workers to move ever faster. Work can eat up the hours of our lives that we need for spiritual reflection, or attitudes we learn at work can stifle our transcendent yearnings, teaching us that only material gain matters or promoting a sense of cynicism that crushes hope. (Interestingly, secular work literature recognizes cynicism as a major symptom of job burnout, which suggests an implicit understanding that healthy people can access hope and transcendence.[16]) Work can harm the relational aspect of our nature in any number of ways: competitive pressure to engage with others as opponents; demanding schedules that leave no time for family and friends; and antisocial working conditions that break down our ability to connect with others. Our work may require us to treat others as objects, even to openly harm them (dealing drugs and running scams are still work, although illegal and immoral), or it may place us in situations where we ourselves are objectified. The theologian Gregory Baum notes that when workers are treated as objects, they can lose the sense that they are subjects, forgetting their own agency and ability to bring about change.[17]

Many working situations fall short of CST's high ideal for work developing the worker in its subjective aspect, and this is another way work can be alienating. Workers can experience alienation when they are "denied participation in the work enterprise," lacking a voice in working conditions and the organization's goals.[18] In general, work can alienate whenever the worker's subjective experience is not considered, "when [work] is organized so as to ensure maximum returns and profits with no concern whether the worker, through [their] own labor, grows or diminishes as a person" (CA 41).

Work that would otherwise be good can become alienating when the conditions surrounding it do not treat workers with the dignity they deserve as human beings. We might imagine someone doing work that is human and creative, where their tasks contribute to the common good and do not objectify others, but the job requires such long hours that the worker has no time for a meaningful human life. For example, a resident doctor exercises her intellectual and caring abilities in treating her patients and knows that her work makes the world a better place, but the demanding hours and low pay might place her at risk for burnout, challenging her mental health and relationships.

Some work, though, is alienating by its very nature, and it's difficult to imagine how such types of work could ever be "salvageable," imaginable as good work, from a Catholic perspective. One such example is sex work, which includes engaging in sexual contact or sexualized performance through pornography, stripping, or social media. From a Catholic perspective, sex work would be considered alienating because of the nature of the work: human sexuality exists to express our relational nature in the context of mutual commitment, not to serve as a commodity for others. No improvements to the stigma, pay, legality, or other working conditions surrounding sex work could make it good work from a Catholic perspective because the work inherently alienates the worker from her relational nature. Thus, sex work is a good test case for whether alienating work can still be considered work, as Tablan denies.

Sex workers, and others who join them in advocating for sex work to be considered work, believe that having what they do be regarded as "work" is the first step in ending the stigma and lack of legal protections that make their lives more dangerous and precarious.[19] These advocates do not claim that sex work is ideal in any respect; many are frank about the dangers inherent in certain types of sex work as well as the fact that workers often choose it as the best of several poor alternatives. I believe Catholic social teaching should support their claim, since in other contexts we do not insist that a particular activity be legal, dignified, or safe in order to recognize it as work.[20] Recognizing bad work as work helps clarify what can be done to move toward the right to dignity for those who do it. In the case of sex work, this might include the destigmatization, legalization, and regulation sex workers advocate for, as well as offering realistic economic alternatives. But seeing this harmful, alienating practice *as work* is what makes it obvious that any response needs to recognize the economic reasons employers offer, and workers do, bad and alienating work.

An example of work that is bad due to its conditions is prison labor, which some refer to as slavery under another name. According to a recent study by the Associated Press, prison laborers grow food, raise and process cattle, and otherwise produce food that ends up in the open-market supply chains of many of the US's best-known food companies. "If they refuse to work, some can jeopardize their chances of parole or face punishment like being sent to solitary confinement. They also are often excluded from protections guaranteed to almost all other full-time workers, even when they are seriously injured or killed on the job,"[21] the AP reporters wrote. While Catholic social teaching would deplore the exploitative conditions in which these inside workers labor, it is clear that what they are doing is work: even work used to exploit people as punishment remains work (*LE* 9). Grouping prison labor with other forms of work allows us to see that corporations do not contract prison laborers to toil in their farms and factories for any reason other than that they have tasks to get done, tasks that only the skills and ingenuity of humans can achieve, and because our laws allow them to offer pennies an hour to incarcerated workers who have no other options.

While work can be alienating due to its inherent nature or its conditions, workers can also alienate themselves. We can use work, intentionally or unintentionally, to distance ourselves from our own human nature. Alienation can occur due to "over-working [or] to work-as-career that often takes on more importance than other human and necessary aspects" (*Compendium* 280). Sometimes we work long hours or hold down multiple jobs out of necessity, for survival. But sometimes, as CST is well aware, people work long hours chasing goals like power, status, or wealth, deemphasizing relationships and community in order to spend more time at work. This could be a way that we use work to alienate ourselves from our human nature. In many situations, workers have little choice but to do bad or alienating work, but sometimes alienation is our own doing.

Pointing out how work can be alienating is rarely intended to blame the worker. Catholic social teaching understands the reality of economic coercion. Workers often realize all too well the way alienating work can harm them, and do not choose alienating work in situations where they have better options. Because many of the ways work can be alienating have to do with working conditions, it's possible to imagine some alienating work turning into good work under more just circumstances. For example, factory workers who must do monotonous tasks can be offered the opportunity to rotate their positions, or a position with punishing hours could have its responsibilities spread across two workers. Housework and childcare can be deeply rewarding for the right person with the right support, or the "problem without a name" women longing for other challenges described to Betty Friedan in the last century. Most often, the label of "alienating" is intended to remind employers of their duty to provide just and safe conditions to their workers, and communities of their responsibility to ensure that every worker can access dignified work that enables their survival. For people who have some choice in their work, avoiding alienation might be a baseline standard, working toward the goal of good work that respects their human nature and develops their abilities.

Along with its high standards for just wages and safe conditions, the Catholic tradition sets a very high bar for the subjective dimension of work. "The entire process of productive work must be adapted to the needs of the person" and workers should be able "to unfold their own abilities and personality through the performance of their work" (*GS 8*). "Work should be the setting for this rich personal growth, where many aspects of life enter into play: creativity, planning for the future, developing our talents, living out our values, relating to others, giving glory to God" (*LS'* 127) and "work should enable the working person to become 'more a human being,' more capable of acting intelligently, freely, and in ways that lead to self-realization."[22] Many of us might feel that at least some of our daily work, paid or unpaid, falls short of this high bar, even if we don't consider our work bad or alienating. Commenting on prison labor, theologian Dwayne David Paul wrote: "If we had the moral and political imagination to see incarcerated people as fellow human beings *and* fellow workers, we'd notice that we lie side-by-side with them on a spectrum of exploitation."[23] Indeed, all work lies on a spectrum from the most just and fulfilling to the most exploitative and alienating. As Paul suggests, recognizing that even the worst working situations create value for employers even as our own work does is an important lesson in solidarity. Recognizing work as work whether it is paid or unpaid, good, bad, or alienating, is how we get there.

Is There Life Beyond Work?

Although work is important for humans—and most of the activities that fill our waking hours can be considered work—Catholic social teaching regards it as equally important to defend the times in our lives when we do something else. Protecting times and spaces where work is not required of us—in a person's weekly routine and across the whole lifespan—has been a part of Catholic social teaching on work since the tradition began. When

Leo XIII called on governments to protect workers' rights—a progressive view at a time when many denied that governments had any right to intervene in the economy—the first right he mentioned was the right not to work on "Sabbath and certain holy days" (*RN* 41). This right is not just for physical rest, but to protect the transcendent part of human nature, our soul, which is called to spend time with God (*RN* 40). Governments should also ensure that working hours and seasons protect human bodies and allow sufficient rest. Protecting rest for body and soul is a sacred duty and the responsibility of both workers and employers: "It is not right to require or to promise the neglect of duties which people owe to God and to themselves" (*RN* 42, my translation). Remember, Catholics view vulnerability as part of human nature. Treating ourselves as vulnerable humans in need of rest, not superhuman machines impervious to breakdown, is living into the truth of who we are as God's creatures, saying "yes" to the way God has made us.

The right to protected time away from work was given more detail in twentieth-century Catholic social teaching documents. All workers have the right to enough time to invest in family, culture, spirituality, and social life, as well as time "freely to develop the energies and potentialities which perhaps they cannot bring to much fruition in their professional work" (*GS* 67). John Paul II defined the right to rest as "a regular weekly rest comprising at least Sunday, and also a longer period of rest, namely the holiday or vacation taken once a year or possibly in several shorter periods during the year" (*LE* 19). The right to rest is a "social benefit" which it is an entire community's job to guarantee. Societies might guarantee the right to rest by requiring employers to provide paid time off or might collectively fund support for workers' retirement—both of which were happening in many developed economies during John Paul II's era.

The Catholic tradition has always argued that people should not have to work until they die, but that communities should create conditions to allow people to work less, giving up any paid labor, at the later end of their lives. Leo XIII strongly defended private property because he understood that for a wage earner, property represented the ability to retire, tend a little plot of land, and live peacefully at the end of life (*RN* 5–7). He envisioned that workers' associations might support members unable to work due to "sickness or old age" (*RN* 57–58). Later, Vatican Council II described economic security for those no longer able to work as the whole community's responsibility: "The livelihood and the human dignity especially of those who are in very difficult conditions because of illness or old age must be guaranteed" (*GS* 66). John Paul II codified this goal into "the right to a pension and to insurance for old age and in case of accidents at work," finding that the ability for everyone to access this right pointed to the justice of an entire economic system (*LE* 19).

Conclusion

Catholic social teaching's inclusive definition of work views it as any activity through which humans use our abilities to transform creation, whether those tasks are paid or unpaid and helpful, harmful, or even alienating to the one who does them. This definition helps us understand how work can be something that we are called to and that is good for us, without the error of thinking that *paid* work is the duty of every adult. Though work is good for us, human dignity does not depend on work. Defining work as purposeful human activity helps us see bad or alienating work as on a continuum with better work, highlighting the economic reasons employers offer it and how we can work to improve it. Though work is good for us, our vulnerable, transcendent human nature deserves protected time away from work, which the church has consistently defended. The remainder of the book will apply this inclusive definition of work as we try to better understand unpaid work as work; how work is good for us; the need for time away from work; and just work compensation and conditions.

Notes

1. Anne Helen Petersen, "Why Office Workers Didn't Unionize," Substack newsletter, *Culture Study* (blog), October 18, 2020, https://annehelen.substack.com/p/why-office-workers-didnt-unionize.
2. Adam Smith, *The Wealth of Nations*, 1776. Available https://www.adamsmithworks.org/documents/cannan-edition, Book V, Chapter 1.
3. Authors of the time, including Victor Hugo, Charles Dickens, and Elizabeth Gaskell, wrote about these concerns in their socially engaged fiction; Leo XIII addresses them in *Rerum Novarum* 36, 42.

4   Malesic, *The End of Burnout*, 76.
5   This translation is from Austin P. Flannery, ed., *Vatican Council II: Constitutions, Decrees, Declarations: The Basic Sixteen Documents*, Revised edition (Collegeville, MN: Liturgical Press, 1996).
6   Karen Cushman, *Catherine, Called Birdy* (New York: Clarion Books, 1995), 13.
7   Cushman, *Catherine, Called Birdy*, 162.
8   This conflation of the duty to work with paid work appears in landmark works by trusted interpreters of Catholic social teaching: Daniel K. Finn, *Christian Economic Ethics: History and Implications* (Minneapolis, MN: Fortress Press, 2013), 339; Thomas Massaro, *Living Justice: Catholic Social Teaching in Action*, 4th ed. (Lanham, MD: Rowman & Littlefield Publishers, 2023), 103; and by the US Conference of Catholic Bishops: US Conference of Catholic Bishops, "A Catholic Framework for Economic Life" (USCCB, 2015, 1996), https://www.usccb.org/resources/catholic-framework-economic-life-0.
9   For much of the history of Catholic social teaching, family caregiving and women's work have been assumed to be nearly interchangeable; see *Rerum Novarum* 42 and *Quadrigesimo Anno* 71. John Paul II and Benedict XVI both treated women working outside the home for pay as a normal part of economic life, and Francis developed Catholic family teaching when he discussed fathers' role in caring for children. See Kate Ward, "Catholic Teaching Changes: Women in the Workplace," *Women In Theology* (blog), August 23, 2019. https://womenintheology.org/2019/08/23/catholic-teaching-changes-women-in-the-workplace/.
10 The fact that some US states require mothers of newborns to be working or looking for work in order to receive cash assistance designated for families is a stark example of this cultural bias against seeing unpaid work as work. Heather Hahn et al., "Work Requirements in Social Safety Net Programs: A Status Report of Work Requirements in TANF, SNAP, Housing Assistance, and Medicaid," *The Urban Institute*, December 2017, https://www.urban.org/sites/default/files/publication/95566/work-requirements-in-social-safety-net-programs.pdf.
11 As Caroline Criado Perez points out, it is far from the case that only historically masculine jobs demand physical strength: "Women working as carers and cleaners can lift more in a shift than a construction worker or a miner." *Invisible Women: Exposing Data Bias in a World Designed for Men* (London: Chatto & Windus, 2019), 114.
12 Hinze, *Glass Ceilings*, 83.
13 Criado Perez, *Invisible Women*, 125–7, 186–91.

14 Tablan, "Catholic Social Teachings," 295.
15 Most US schoolkids learn that Henry Ford revolutionized factory production by introducing the assembly line. I was in my forties before I learned that this monotonous, uncreative work was so distasteful to a workforce accustomed to exercising their own ingenuity on the job that Ford was forced to double the wage of a daily laborer to get enough workers for his assembly lines. Matthew B. Crawford, *Shop Class as Soulcraft: An Inquiry into the Value of Work* (New York: Penguin Press, 2009), 41–3.
16 Malesic, *The End of Burnout*, 20–5.
17 Gregory Baum, *The Priority of Labor: A Commentary on Laborem Exercens: Encyclical Letter of Pope John Paul II* (Mahwah, NJ: Paulist Press, 1982), 15.
18 Patricia A. Lamoureux, "Commentary on Laborem Exercens (On Human Works)," in *Modern Catholic Social Teaching: Commentaries and Interpretations*, ed. Kenneth R. Himes (Washington, DC: Georgetown University Press, 2005), 410.
19 Grant, *Playing the Whore*, 56.
20 Kate Ward, "Human and Alienating Work: What Sex Worker Advocates Can Teach Catholic Social Thought," *Journal of the Society of Christian Ethics* 41, no. 2 (2021): 261–78, https://doi.org/10.5840/jsce2021112952.
21 Robin McDowell and Margie Mason, "Prisoners in the US Are Part of a Hidden Workforce Linked to Hundreds of Popular Food Brands," *Associated Press*, January 29, 2024, https://apnews.com/article/prison-to-plate-inmate-labor-investigation-c6f0eb4747963283316e494eadf08c4e.
22 U.S. Conference of Catholic Bishops, "Economic Justice for All: Pastoral Letter on Catholic Social Teaching and the U.S. Economy," 1986, para. 72, http://www.usccb.org/upload/economic_justice_for_all.pdf.
23 Dwayne David Paul, "A.P. Prison Labor Report Reveals More about Workers than Prisons," *Religion in Revolt*, February 16, 2024, https://www.religionrevolt.org/latest/ap-prison-labor-report-reveals-more-about-work-than-prisons.

3

Caregiving:

Is It Work If You Love Them?

Chapter Outline

Care Work in Catholic Social Teaching	43
Care as Skilled Labor	45
Why Don't We Value Care?	50
The Economic Value of Unpaid Care	53
Justice for Unpaid Caregivers	56
Conclusion	58

When I started teaching, the idea that unpaid tasks could be work struck many of my students as entirely new. Once our class had covered Catholic social teaching's inclusive definition of work as any useful, rational human activity, we'd wrestle together with what this meant for unpaid work, like care given within the family. We all agreed that unpaid care is important; after all, we all begin life receiving care from someone. Giving unpaid care—whether to kids, older parents, loved ones with disabilities, other family members, or friends—is part of what most of us see as a well-lived adult life. But what does it mean to see this care as *work*?[1] Does that mean work isn't necessarily something bad? Are we working for ourselves when we cook our own dinner? Things only got more confusing when we remembered that according to Catholic social teaching, even unpaid work comes with rights to just compensation. One student puzzled, "Does this mean I should be paying my wife to take care of our daughter?"

Many folks today find it challenging to think of unpaid care as work. We might feel that unpaid care is something different from work—more noble or enjoyable—because it is done out of love or even "naturally" (more on this later). Or we think of work as busy, important, and onerous—building bridges, making money—and overlook the skill and effort that care requires. Most of us don't really think that care is unimportant or always easy. But in a sense, that's what we're saying when we dismiss those who keep house or take care of their own kids by saying they "don't work." Catholic social teaching's inclusive definition of work allows us to recognize that many forms of work are done out of love, while still remaining work, with its joys, challenges, and potential to transform us.

Catholic social teaching finds common ground with many contemporary thinkers on feminism and families: unpaid care is work. Today, this idea is becoming better known. An ongoing conversation about couples learning to fairly share housework and childcare makes it clear that these tasks are *work*, not fun leisure activities or a woman's natural bodily functions. Sociologist Arlie Russell Hochschild put unpaid work in familiar paid-work terms when she dubbed housework and family care "the second shift" in her book of the same name. By popularizing the label "adulting" for mundane daily tasks, online millennials did their part to make that labor visible.[2] Finally, the Covid-19 pandemic served as rocket fuel to the conversation. With schools and daycares closed, parents who were able to work from home had the paid job, the childcare, the laundry, and dinner all happening in the same space (and frequently at the same time). Because of this, in the United States, federal support for childcare was discussed more seriously than it had been since President Nixon vetoed a childcare bill in 1971.[3] As I wrote this chapter, both major political parties in the 2024 US presidential election added childcare funding proposals to their platforms. We've come a long way toward seeing unpaid care as work, to the point that advocates now call for governments to pay caregivers in compensation for the work they do.

Feminist activists in the United States called for government support for unpaid home labor as early as the 1920s.[4] Today, the idea is practically trendy. Multiple recent books from feminist writers uphold the goodness of care and its importance to the whole society, challenging the misunderstanding that care is a private, individual choice. But Catholic social teaching came to this insight long ago. Since the earliest documents of Catholic social teaching in 1891, the popes referred to unpaid care work in the same breath as they discussed the work of paid workers. While Leo XIII and Pius XI assumed that all unpaid caregivers were women, they frankly spoke of unpaid care as work, including it when they discussed realities affecting work in their time and calling for just treatment of paid and unpaid workers alike. By recognizing care as work, the early framers of Catholic social teaching avoided sentimentalizing unpaid caregiving, at a time when many in the United States and Europe saw women's role as limited to the "angel in the house." More recent Popes acknowledged fathers' roles in family caregiving and outlined specific models for government financial support of care, including family grants and universal basic income. From its beginning to today, Catholic social teaching has insisted on care work's importance to the flourishing of entire communities and caregivers' right to expect dignity and a stable livelihood.[5]

Care Work in Catholic Social Teaching

In 1931, Pope Pius XI wrote *Quadragesimo Anno* (*QA*), an encyclical honoring the forty-year anniversary of *Rerum Novarum* and observing what had changed and what had not for worker justice since that 1891 encyclical. *QA* describes women's at-home, unpaid labor as work and more clearly restates a point Leo XIII had already made in 1891: since wealth originates from workers' labor, all workers have a right to share in its profits to a degree that allows them to enjoy a secure and stable life (*QA* 53). Today, many still find it radical to claim that unpaid care is work and entitles the caregiver to a stable livelihood drawn from community wealth. But these ideas were already present in the work of the early CST framers.

John Paul II further fleshed out and detailed the dignity and importance of unpaid care labor in his 1981 encyclical on work, *Laborem Exercens*. Like especially challenging forms of traditionally male labor, care work can be "toilsome":

> Toil is something that is universally known, for it is universally experienced. It is familiar to those doing physical work under sometimes exceptionally laborious conditions. It is familiar not only to agricultural workers, who

spend long days working the land . . . but also to those who work in mines and quarries, to steel-workers at their blast-furnaces, to those who work in builders' yards and in construction work. . . . It is familiar to women, who, sometimes without proper recognition on the part of society and even of their own families, bear the daily burden and responsibility for their homes and the upbringing of their children. *It is familiar to all workers* and, since work is a universal calling, it is familiar to everyone. (*LE* 9)

Not only did the twentieth-century Pope recognize unpaid care as work, he saw it as an important example of how work can be good for us and still difficult, along with such clearly "toilsome" professions as farming, building, and mining. Furthermore, understanding unpaid care as work was key to understanding what work means in our lives. "The work of women in the home [must] be recognized and respected by all in its irreplaceable value. . . . All people, in every area, are working with equal rights and equal responsibilities" (*Familiaris Consortio* 23).

Today we roll our eyes at the assumption that all women are caregivers and all caregivers are women, which seems to be present in these Catholic social teaching documents. It's worth noting that John Paul II had no desire to "send all women back to the home"; he advocated that women should work in every sphere of public life (*LE* 19, *FC* 23).[6] He insisted that fathers' role in their families is not just as provider but as an active, involved parent and teacher of the children (*FC* 25). Certainly, it was an oversight on his part to identify unpaid care only with the work of women. That oversight should not distract us from the significance of the tradition's insistence that unpaid family care is work, equal in importance with building, mining, and science. Several interlinked ideas can be seen in this consistent message: those who give care, and those who need it, are important; there is more to life than what makes money; all work is equal in dignity, whether paid or unpaid; and women and men are equal in dignity and rights.

Pope Francis's teaching on behalf of the Church acknowledged what many families already knew from experience: unpaid family care work is not only done by women. He published *Amoris Laetitia*, "On Love in the Family," following a series of meetings where church leaders and family experts from all over the world reported on their experience of the joys and challenges of family life.[7] "Masculinity and femininity are not rigid categories," Francis wrote in this document. "It is possible, for example, that a husband's way of being masculine can be flexibly adapted to the wife's work schedule. Taking on domestic chores or some aspects of raising children does not make him any less masculine or imply failure, irresponsibility or cause for shame" (*AL* 286). Despite some confusion of categories (what can it mean for masculinity, a gendered characteristic of a person, to be adapted to anyone's work schedule?), with *Amoris Laetitia*, the Church's teaching explicitly clarified what Catholics have long known: unpaid family caregiving is a reality in families of many configurations, and men can excel at it as well as women. Care is work, and deserves dignity, no matter who does it.

For Catholic teaching, some of the questions raised by recognizing unpaid care as work are not really inconsistencies. Work is a good thing for us, so it's not a contradiction that caring for loved ones could also be work. Even the idea that unpaid caregivers should be paid is not radical from a Catholic perspective. Recently, economists and politicians have developed elaborate arguments for paying caregivers. But it's been obvious to papal framers since the inception of CST that unpaid care is work, work that is crucial to a community's flourishing, and if unpaid caregivers can't support themselves, society has a duty and a vested interest in financially supporting their labor. The CST framers see these points as fairly obvious and don't spend a lot of time supporting them in detail. We can understand these insights more fully by learning from other experts on care: sociologists, economists, and caregivers themselves.

Care as Skilled Labor

During the Covid-19 pandemic, author Angela Garbes published *Essential Labor*, my favorite of several recent books taking unpaid family care seriously as work—from its importance to society, to its impact on the caregiver, to the ways larger forces like immigration policy shape the ways we give and receive care. Far from innate or automatic, doing care work well requires using our body, mind, and spirit and a store of knowledge gained throughout a lifetime. We rely on what we've learned, implicitly and explicitly, from others' perspectives on how to care, and the knowledge of what the cared-for one needs that only comes from an intimate relationship. Garbes reminds us that much of caregiving consists of what she calls "maintenance labor": along with direct physical and emotional help, caregiving involves a lot of planning and preparing the environment where the cared-for one will be safe and nurtured. Meal preparation, laundry, and cleaning; making and carrying out social plans; and managing prescriptions and doctor's appointments are all commonplace parts of caregiving that require a variety of manual, mental, and long-range planning skills.[8] And this skilled work can be carried out regardless of the worker's feelings for the one receiving care. Theologian Christine Firer Hinze distinguishes the *tasks* of care work from the spontaneous *feeling* of care or love for the cared-for one: "Practicing care involves responding morally, actively, appropriately, and reliably to the other's need. Care relationships require such responses whether or not the caregiver is actively drawn to the work to be done."[9]

"Care work" is also something we do for ourselves, odd though it may sound. The labor of making meals, doing laundry, and keeping things clean has to get done, whether we do it ourselves or pay someone else. My college students most often don't have dependents, but they perform significant acts of care work for each other: roommates cook each other dinner, and friends devote significant emotional effort to supporting each other through life's challenges. Young people starting a first full-time job are sometimes surprised by how many hours in the day, after work, are eaten up by grocery shopping, preparing meals, and caring for the home and our bodily needs—in other words, the unpaid care work we do for ourselves. Some preserve time for paid work by outsourcing as many "maintenance tasks" as possible, while others find that friendships and family relationships falter without putting time into maintaining those connections. Catholic social teaching's definition of work as including both paid and unpaid tasks accurately reflects many people's experiences: No wonder that we feel overwhelmed when, after working a full day, we have little choice but to return home and do more work.

As challenging as our own care work tasks can be, the burden of unpaid care is multiplied for those who are expected to care for others without compensation, simply on the basis of who they are. Historically and still today, women and girls have been expected to shoulder the majority of unpaid care work, which limits other opportunities available to them. As Hinze points out, unpaid care work limits the time available for paid work, along with caregivers' ability to accumulate savings and the power and security that come with financial assets. Since unpaid care work is poorly respected and regarded as "natural" to women, it also transfers this low status to paid caregivers, who are often undercompensated for the complex skills they use in their labor because employers expect them to do their paid labor "out of love."[10]

If we see care work as "natural," we might think that it is easy or spontaneous, or does not demand much from the caregiver. On the contrary, care work demands evolving attention and skill, drawing on all the caregiver's resources: spiritual, mental, emotional, and, of course, physical. As Garbes observes:

> The only way a young child can comprehend love is physically . . . drool wiping, hand washing, nose blowing, food spooning, hair brushing, bathing, picking up, putting down to put clothes on, changing diapers. . . . You have to show children [love] with physical attention and affection. And you have to show them over and over and over again.[11]

Though profoundly physical, care work is not automatic, but demands attunement to the cared-for one's needs and mental energy to respond to their needs appropriately as they evolve, along with everything else that needs to be done. As attorney and writer Ivana Greco observes, "The most useful tool I have in dealing with a toddler throwing a tantrum, or with how to cook three dishes needing different temperatures in one oven, is not an app or a gadget—it is my own brain."[12]

As well as reasoning, advance planning, and logistics, caregivers must be experts in a skill sociologist Arlie Hochschild calls emotional labor: when workers are required to maintain a specific emotion in themselves or other people as part of the conditions of their work. Emotional labor "requires one to induce or suppress feeling in order to sustain the outward countenance that produces the proper state of mind in others."[13] "Emotional labor" is sometimes used to refer to any invisible or unappreciated labor, such as maintaining family social obligations, but Hochschild believes it is worthwhile to keep its intended focus on the feelings.[14] This helps us see how emotional labor carries a unique risk: manipulating one's own emotions as a job requirement can "estrange or alienate" the worker from her own emotions over time.[15]

When emotional labor is part of a paid job, workers must cede control of their emotions—one of the most intimate parts of human selfhood—to their employer's preferences.[16] For example, Hochschild attended the training program for Delta flight attendants, who were given specific training in what emotions to project (always smile), how to manage the emotions of others (make passengers feel important and right, even if they are behaving badly), and even how to interact with fellow flight attendants out of public view (don't vent about difficult passengers, as it spreads the bad mood around.)[17] The job requirement to display positive emotions and suppress negative ones consistently and on command sometimes damaged flight attendants' ability to experience and interpret their own feelings, even off the job.[18] Hochschild also studied bill collectors, whose employers, in contrast, encouraged them to be aggressive, to find ways to undermine debtors' self-image, and assume that all debtors belonged to a separate, dishonest class of people.[19] Both groups of workers found that the specific emotions their job required them to perform—relational qualities and charm for flight attendants, anger and defensiveness for bill collectors—became more difficult for them to experience at appropriate times when they were no longer on the job.[20] The requirement to use emotions on command at work "alienated," or distanced, these workers from a normal experience of their own human feelings.

When you are a caregiver, there may not be a boss telling you how to manage your emotions, but emotional work, as Hochschild calls emotional labor when it's not done for pay, is clearly a crucial skill in the toolbox.[21] The volunteer community leader who manages to convey hope and pride to her group after a disappointing setback, or the parent who stays calm and positive while wrangling a toddler tantrum, may not be doing emotional labor (for pay), but they are doing emotional work. Managing our own emotions—the anger at a teenager's rudeness, sadness at an elder's diminishing abilities, or frustration with a friend who wants to vent about the same problems yet again—is part of the emotional labor of care, too.

As with work in general, calling something emotional labor does not mean we are saying it's a bad thing to do or unjust that we must do it. Hochschild details how much meaning and enjoyment some workers find in jobs that require emotional labor, even those that might strike others as unbearably difficult, like working in a hospice.[22] Few of us would give up the intimacy and trust that can result from the emotional work we put in while giving care to dependents or friends. Hochschild's research shows us how managing our own and others' emotions is not automatic, easy, or "natural," but requires considerable attention and skill. Acknowledging that the management of our own and others' emotions that caregiving requires is indeed work may help us better understand why this work is challenging and appreciate it more fully.

Another concept that helps us understand unpaid care as work is "connective labor," which sociologist Alison Pugh defines as "the forging of an emotional understanding with another person to create valuable outcomes."[23] This work involves "empathic listening, in which one cultivates a sense or a vision of the other person, and witnessing, in which that vision is reflected back to the other . . . Most important, this process is deeply interactive, not least because for connective labor to land successfully, the other must assent—to some degree—with the vision that is being reflected their way."[24] Clearly, not all care labor is connective labor. Food preparation, laundry, and filling prescriptions are all important care tasks that do not involve forging a connection with another person. But caregivers will readily recognize how getting an overtired child to bed, encouraging a teenager to act responsibly, or supporting an elder through life transitions involves the skilled and delicate forging of an emotional connection.

I especially appreciate how Pugh's definition of connective labor shows us how this type of work is interactive, even mutual. Caring for another person is not the same as acting upon a physical object whose properties are predictable and knowable. Whether we are particularly skilled at it or not, care is always a dynamic process of responding to the other person in the moment. For example, the physical movements of changing a diaper are relatively simple and consistent, but the experience for caregiver and baby will be very different depending on whether the baby is tired, hungry, or giggly, a fragile newborn or an active toddler. A skilled caregiver makes the task easier on herself by reading the baby's emotions and responding to what she sees as the baby's need for quiet or play. Keeping an energetic child in place during a messy diaper change can challenge a strong adult, but emotional and connective labor, skillfully deployed, can lessen the physical labor required. Multiply this skilled, consistent emotional attunement by every task the caregiver needs to perform, and we can see the truth of Pugh's observation that connective labor undergirds much of the benefits humans gain from life in society. Like emotional labor, connective labor is important to many employers who will hire and pay for this complex skill. We profoundly undervalue the complex skills involved in care when we assume that the ability to do it well is "natural" or innate for some people and inevitably more difficult for others.

Understanding the mental and emotional complexity involved in doing care work well helps us better appreciate care as work. Remember that for

Catholic social teaching, the most important part of work is always its subjective element, how work transforms the worker. Many caregivers find it easy to identify how their caregiving has changed them as people, in helpful and perhaps harmful ways. As caregivers work through physical, mental, emotional, and connective labor to keep their charges healthy in body, mind, and spirit, they develop their own capacities for patience, creativity, and attunement to others' needs. At the same time, care work can override our attention to our own needs and occupy the mental space we might prefer to use for other tasks. "Physical [care] labor exhausts me, but it makes me more tender," Garbes writes.[25] Like many caregivers, journalist Elissa Strauss found that the demands of care forced her to be more honest with herself about her own needs and limits.[26] For many adults, caregiving is one of the most self-transformative things they will ever do. Understanding care as work helps us appreciate its skilled nature, its subjective element, and its significant value to society.

Why Don't We Value Care?

While our society struggles to see unpaid care as work and to value it in the same way paid work is respected, this was not always the case. Before the Industrial Revolution, and still today in less industrialized settings, producing goods for the market mostly took place within households. Even as men and women may have performed different tasks, both saw themselves as engaged in the labor of providing for the family. The shift to factory production led to today's common understanding that "work" is something that is done outside the home, for wages, and traditionally only by men. (This understanding of "work" ignores the fact that paid work outside the home had always been an economic necessity for many women, in some cases because of legal frameworks that pushed marginalized women out of their own homes and into poorly paid labor—as has been the case for generations of immigrant and African American women in the United States.[27])

Hinze details how this historical shift from in-home to waged work accompanied a change in the understanding of family care. "The modern breadwinner-homemaker division reflected a dual-spheres ideology that accorded public value to paid labor, and redefined male economic success . . . as the ability to support a family through wages. . . . Occurring in the so-called private realm, homemakers' contributions were considered noneconomic."[28] As cash income became necessary for families' survival in modern times, "noneconomic" became synonymous with "less important." This is how communities began to see care as something other than work, failing to appreciate its difficulty and importance and the contributions and skills of the workers, mostly women, who were doing it. Work—men's tasks—was seen as important and as mentally or physically difficult, while care was barely considered a task but simply a "natural" function of women.

Today, women and girls do more than three-quarters of unpaid care work globally.[29] This discrepancy eats into the time caregivers can spend earning money or getting an education, with the global average for women being 4.5 hours of unpaid care work per day, compared to the less than 90 minutes men contribute.[30] This gender discrepancy is a problem, but not because there is something harmful about care work in itself; these tasks are important and need to get done. But it is harmful when women and girls are expected to do unpaid care work to an extent that interferes with their ability to survive in economies that depend on education and waged labor.

When we see care work as easy, or as not even work at all, because it is "natural," we undervalue both the work itself and those who do it. Disrespect for care work contributes to sexist attitudes against women and girls, who are seen as "natural" caregivers, and upholds the status quo in which care work earns no monetary compensation from society, keeping caregivers impoverished compared to other workers. Of course, it's true that work—including care work—is natural to *all* humans. Catholic thought sees human nature as loving, creative, and interdependent, so it's part of our nature to care for one another and to join together in groups to apply reason to solving problems. But that doesn't mean we are born knowing how to run a commercial kitchen, write a TV script, or drill for oil. We rightly recognize that these forms of work depend on the skills workers acquire through explicit instruction from others and through their own experience. By recognizing care as work, Catholic social teaching cues us to see it as skilled and important, and to value, respect, and fairly compensate paid and unpaid caregivers.

Not only are caregivers less respected in many communities; so are those in need of care. Hochschild suggests that "part of what makes care work invisible is that the people the worker cares for—children, the elderly, the disabled—are themselves somewhat invisible."[31] Indeed, it seems to me that part of the devaluation of care work rests in a cultural distaste for people whose vulnerabilities require care: children, the sick, those with disabilities, and older adults. US culture envisions the free, happy person as one who is independent, not needing anyone, and able to do whatever she wants on her own. To need help from anyone else is seen as embarrassing, lessening someone's dignity. Theologian Michele Saracino explains how the dominant culture forms people in "the mentality that the best way to be human is to surpass limits, overcome barriers, and be independent to an extreme—to not need. This is why being called needy can be so painful. We learn that our neediness conflicts with the social norm to be in control of everything."[32] Widespread cultural distaste for vulnerability stands firmly at odds with Christian theology, which insists that persons in need of help, vulnerable persons, are precious and valued in the sight of God, as they should be in our own. Christians believe that Jesus came to us as a fragile newborn baby and died a violent death, helpless before the Roman Empire. If God can become vulnerable, our call is not to despise the vulnerable people among us, but to respond with loving care.

Responding to others' needs is not only good for those we help, Christian theology believes, it is good for those who help, as well. Beginning with the Bible, the "Christian tradition maintains that human beings are, by nature, social beings that can develop fully only in relationships with others. . . . People develop into their true selves only when they are able to give of themselves to others in 'a sincere gift of self,' as John Paul II frequently taught," theologian Mary Doak explains.[33] Shane Clifton, a theologian who became quadriplegic in adulthood, observes that acceptance of necessary assistance can help disabled people develop the virtue of humility, understood theologically as "giving in to grace."[34] He observes that humility is an even more necessary virtue for those with power and advises caregivers to accept the limits of their knowledge and collaborate with the cared-for one.[35] Care is not a one-way street, but a process of mutual learning between the caregiver and the cared-for, which helps them both grow more fully into their nature as relational human beings.

The Economic Value of Unpaid Care

For Catholic social teaching, the connection between care and the formal economy has always been clear: both unpaid care and wage-earning outside the home are work, and both complement each other. "*Connecting, upholding, giving* and *receiving* come before, undergird, and are essential to the purposes of *working, gaining, mastering, getting, spending,* or *keeping*," as Hinze summarizes CST's view. "No one individuates, competes, creates, or accomplishes who does not simultaneously receive, relate with, and depend upon *care*."[36] The CST documents rarely bother to explicitly spell out that the formal economy relies on care, which the tradition sees as fairly obvious. From a Catholic perspective, care work is self-evidently work because it's a way humans use our skills to shape and transform the world around us, and it's self-evidently valuable because it provides a service that is necessary to healthy human lives and communities. Catholic thought does not need to assign a dollar value to care in order to see it as important, but for some commentators, this helps. Pointing to the economic value of unpaid care can encourage the broader community to respect it and make the case for why societies should pay family caregivers.

The traditional economic definition of work limits it to tasks done for pay, which author Leah Libresco Sargeant points out as an arbitrary distinction that has more to do with what economists can easily count than with human experience. "If only wage work is seen as 'real' work, then a father who stays home with his young children doesn't count as providing for his family," she wrote. "If the father swaps kids with a neighbor and each family pays the other to take care of its kids, then the same diaper changes, food preparation and reading of storybooks become official work."[37] Acknowledging this truth does not even require us to view unpaid care as particularly important work, just to accept the logic that the tasks are the same whether or not a worker is paid. But in an effort to highlight the importance of unpaid care, many feminists point out that every activity traditional economics does "count"—everything that earns pay or creates profit—is ultimately made possible by unpaid care and caregivers.

One of the first attempts to draw attention to the economic contribution of care work was made by an international feminist movement called Wages for Housework in the 1970s.[38] These activists sought to show the connection between unpaid home labor and profit-making production.[39] A 1973 flyer from the New York arm of the group read, "Married or not, with or without children, holding a paid job or not, we are expected to make people's lives more bearable—one's own or someone else's.... What would happen without us laboring to get everybody ready for work, without us raising the future workers? Government, industry and everything else would stop functioning."[40] More recently, advocates of support for families providing at-home child care during the Covid-19 pandemic rallied to the claim that "child care is infrastructure." Just like the bridges, roads, and utilities more commonly referred to that way, child care needs to be in place in order for other economic activity to continue, as many workers found when Covid school closures disrupted business as usual. The prefix *infra* refers to the base of a structure, and indeed, societies are built on a foundation of care given to young children, who take their place as shapers of their communities—running businesses, providing health care, and doing all the other work a community needs—only after they have first received care.

Some scholars give care work a more clearly economic label by dubbing it "reproductive labor," that is, the work that reproduces human bodies or societies, supplying the food, rest, and other goods humans need to survive, as well as the social bonds and connections that keep communities alive.[41] Biological reproduction—carrying and bearing children—is not understood as labor in this theory, but caring for babies and children definitely is. This kind of work is also "reproductive" because it must be constantly reproduced—done again and again, day in and day out. Scholars use this term in order to point out that the "productive labor" that creates goods and earns money depends for its existence on reproductive labor, or care. As feminist philosopher Nancy Fraser wrote, "Unwaged social reproductive activity is necessary to the existence of waged work, the accumulation of surplus value, and the functioning of capitalism as such. None of these things could exist in the absence of housework, child-raising, schooling, affective care, and a host of other activities that serve to produce new generations of workers and replenish existing ones, as well as to maintain social bonds and shared understandings. Social reproduction is an indispensable background condition for the possibility of economic production in a capitalist society."[42]

"Wages for housework" and "reproductive labor" proclaim the value of care work by putting it in terms widely understood in our capitalist society, describing care in the same language as work that earns wages. A popular Internet meme created by a payroll software company makes the same point. Breaking down the work of a "stay-at-home mom" into job categories like "dietitian," "facilities director" and "psychologist," Salary.com calculated the fair market value of a stay-at-home mom's labor at $178,201 yearly—more than the average dentist earns.[43] As these memes circulate online, they often seem to be shared by family caregivers—mostly mothers without full-time paid jobs—who recognize a sense of pride in the view that their skills, on the open market, could be seen to command such high pay. Far from insisting that their work is "priceless" because it is done out of love, caregivers who share this meme find self-respect when their work is valued in economic terms.

As well as coming up with individual dollar values for a care worker, advocates have tried to calculate the market value of care work in the aggregate. If unpaid care work were paid at the local minimum wage, it would contribute $10 trillion to the global economy, making it an industry three times the size of the tech sector.[44] Specific care practices can also be given a dollar value as a way to argue for their importance. For example, researchers estimate that "the breast milk produced in Australia," where their study was conducted, contributes $4 billion in value to the economy there, more than the baby food industry. These researchers make the point that the labor and time that goes into breastfeeding babies is not supported by government subsidies—as food industries often are—or counted into a nation's GDP.[45]

Not only is care usually uncompensated by the communities that benefit from the unpaid labor, but providing care actually strips earning power from caregivers. Given that unpaid care cuts into the caregiver's opportunities to make money and build wealth, even as it contributes to the formal economy where others make their money, Hinze says,

> The time and energy (physical, emotional, and intellectual) expended by those doing household and care work create a hidden transfer from these workers' pockets, clocks and lives to the pockets, clocks and lives of those who benefit from their cheap, or free, labor . . . a tax paid daily by everyone who engages in unpaid or paid care work.[46]

When advocates call for societies to support unpaid care workers financially, they are trying to recognize the significant financial value care work contributes to societies and to pay back the "hidden transfer" of value from unpaid caregivers to the rest of us. (We will talk more about specific proposals for what this financial support might look like in Chapter 6.) Insisting that care is work, or pointing to the fact that it might deserve wages, makes the case that this work has value in a society that tends to value only things that can be given a price. Catholic thought sees care as valuable because it is work that shapes the worker; because it cares for precious bodies of vulnerable human beings; and because it sustains life—all things of great value in Catholic thought, but valueless in the formal economy. Outside of Catholic thought, framings that put unpaid care in economic terms—like Wages for Housework and reproductive labor—try to put the value of unpaid care in terms where mainstream economic thought can understand its worth.

Justice for Unpaid Caregivers

Too often, when care work is presented as a challenge, it is framed as a challenge to individual families, where parents employed outside the home struggle to balance their home responsibilities with their paid jobs. (And most often, this is presented as a problem for women who cannot manage to "have it all.") Solutions are offered, such as outsourcing the care labor or eliminating some of it, for example, "lowering one's standards" in terms of child care or home cleanliness. But as Hinze points out, shifting women's labor from inside the home to outside it, by involving more women in the paid workforce, does not resolve the challenges care work poses. Someone still needs to do the care labor, and if it is outsourced to a paid caregiver, the problems of low pay and low respect will just become hers instead.[47]

Government proposals to help families with care labor fall short when they take too prescriptive an approach to what families should look like or how they should accomplish their care labor. For example, some proposals are designed to push parents of young children into the paid workforce, while others would reward biological parents (envisioned as mostly mothers) who stay home with their own children. An adequate public care policy would recognize the fact that families come in many forms. Researcher Amber Lapp, writing for the conservative US think tank American Compass, noted that family support policies that only benefit married couples or families with an employed adult exclude those most in need of help, effectively penalizing poor children for family circumstances they are helpless to change.[48] A family care policy that follows the cues of Catholic social teaching would support women and men equally whether they remain in the paid workforce or provide unpaid care at home, would allow for transitions between paid work and unpaid care, would support families of any structure, and would provide for needs related to elder care and care of dependent adults as well.

As I mentioned, we will say more about compensation for unpaid care in Chapter 6. Catholic social teaching sees paid and unpaid work as essentially similar, and just compensation for both as the job of entire societies, not individuals or families. Since it is work, unpaid care work should have working conditions that are adequate to the worker's dignity. This chapter will close with a word about those conditions.

My student joked about paying his wife to take care of their daughter; of course, most families would find it unrealistic to have one wage-earner compensate other family members for unpaid care. However, there is a sense in which unpaid caregivers' family members, especially their spouses, influence the caregivers' working conditions. Responsibilities for unpaid work in the home—chores and childcare—have never remotely approached parity between male and female partners, even when the female partner works full time outside the home; on average, men perform less than 30 percent of the total unpaid household tasks.[49] In some families, the spouse who works for pay gets most of the weekend "off" from family tasks, enjoying free time while the caregiving spouse continues doing unpaid labor. Catholic social teaching's inclusive definition of work allows us to clearly see these situations as unjust. Sheryl Sandberg, the tech executive and expert on workplace gender equality, famously advised that "as more women lean in to their careers, more men need to lean in to their families," urging men to take on their fair share of care work so their wives can advance professionally.[50] When we see unpaid care as work, we can recognize that it's not just professional advancement at stake—inequality in unpaid caregiving is work injustice.

Reflecting on gender inequality in family care work, Arlie Hochschild referenced "alienation"—a term used in both Catholic thought and her own field of sociology—to describe work that separates workers from their own nature. She proposed that unpaid care work can quickly become alienating when unequal expectations assign all of this work to one partner, usually the woman. "The solution is not for men and women to share alienated work," she advised, "the solution is for men and women to share enchanted [that is, rewarding] work. These are expressions of love."[51] Care work, emotional labor, and connective labor may be labor, but that does not mean they have to be inevitably, permanently burdensome or alienating. Like all work, care work can be fulfilling and meaningful; it can develop the worker's skills and express her sense of self. Recognizing unpaid care for what it is—work—helps us see more clearly the conditions that can help grant this ubiquitous, underappreciated, crucially important labor the recognition and dignity the workers who do it deserve.

Conclusion

This chapter has argued that care is work—skilled, challenging work that is part of everyone's life, regardless of gender. The economy we all depend on is upheld by the unpaid care work done for ourselves and our families and friends. Insisting that care is work and that unpaid care has a measurable economic impact is not intended to cheapen care by reducing it to a marketable commodity. Rather, it helps show how poorly economic thinking measures what matters in life, and allows us to call on communities and governments to support this work without making appeals to its intrinsic value that all members of society might not share. Catholic social teaching's perspective is clear: care is work, and like all work, it deserves respect and recognition from the community and compensation that allows the worker to live a dignified life.

Notes

1. Of course, many people do care work as a paid job. This chapter focuses on unpaid care as an example that helps us unpack how CST's definition of work can apply to unpaid work. Hinze, *Glass Ceilings*, is an excellent exploration of the similarities and overlaps between paid and unpaid care work, and ethical issues surrounding both.
2. Julie Beck, "When Do You Become an Adult?," *The Atlantic* (blog), January 5, 2016, https://www.theatlantic.com/health/archive/2016/01/when-are-you-really-an-adult/422487/.

3   Kate Ward, "America's Child Care Crisis and Catholic Social Teaching," *America Magazine*, October 2021, https://www.americamagazine.org/politics-society/2021/09/16/childcare-work-catholic-social-teaching-241381.
4   Silvia Federici and Arlen Austin, *The New York Wages for Housework Committee 1972–1977: History, Theory and Documents* (New York: Autonomedia, 2017), 12.
5   On the romanticization of women's unpaid home work, see Hinze, *Glass Ceilings*, 66–69.
6   For a fuller evaluation of Laborem Exercens' legacy on gender, see Christine Firer Hinze, "Women, Families, and the Legacy of 'Laborem Exercens': An Unfinished Agenda," *Journal of Catholic Social Thought* 6, no. 1 (2009): 63–92. Hinze writes that this encyclical is "not a 'send all women back to the home' agenda. It is, however, a genderkeyed interpretation that sees women as especially suited to and needed in the work of home and family, and also having a distinct, feminine contribution to make to culture and society" (80).
7   The technical term for this kind of Church teaching document is "post-synodal apostolic exhortation." Synods, in the Catholic context, are meetings of the global Church.
8   Angela Garbes, *Essential Labor: Mothering as Social Change* (New York: Harper Wave, 2022), 74–81.
9   Hinze, *Glass Ceilings*, 12.
10 Hinze, *Glass Ceilings*, 88–90.
11 Garbes, *Essential Labor*, 68, 71.
12 Ivana Greco, "When We Outsource Every Hard Thing, What Do We Lose?," *Public Discourse*, July 18, 2024, https://www.thepublicdiscourse.com/2024/07/95423/.
13 Arlie Russell Hochschild, *The Managed Heart: Commercialization of Human Feeling*, 3rd ed., EBSCO Academic Collection Ebooks (Berkeley, CA: University of California Press, 2012), 7.
14 Julie Beck, "The Concept Creep of 'Emotional Labor,'" *The Atlantic* (blog), November 26, 2018, https://www.theatlantic.com/family/archive/2018/11/arlie-hochschild-housework-isnt-emotional-labor/576637/.
15 Hochschild, *The Managed Heart*, 7.
16 Hochschild, *The Managed Heart*, 119.
17 Hochschild, *The Managed Heart*, chapter 6.
18 Hochschild, *The Managed Heart*, 21.
19 Hochschild, *The Managed Heart*, 143–7.
20 Hochschild, *The Managed Heart*, 164.

21 Hochschild, *The Managed Heart*, 7.
22 Arlie Russell Hochschild, "Can Emotional Labor Be Fun?," in *So How's the Family?: And Other Essays*, ed. Arlie Russell Hochschild (Oakland, CA: University of California Press, 2013), https://doi.org/10.1525/california/9780520272279.003.0003.
23 Allison J. Pugh, *The Last Human Job: The Work of Connecting in a Disconnected World* (Princeton, NJ: Princeton University Press, 2024), 16.
24 Pugh, *The Last Human Job*, 17.
25 Garbes, *Essential Labor*, 71.
26 Elissa Strauss, *When You Care: The Unexpected Magic of Caring for Others* (New York: Gallery Books, 2024), 165.
27 Premilla Nadasen, *Care: The Highest Stage of Capitalism* (Chicago, IL: Haymarket Books, 2023), chapter 3. Throughout US history, for example, laws, policies, and practices have directed African American, Puerto Rican, and Indigenous people into domestic work, as well as Irish immigrants during a historical period when they were understood as non-white.
28 Hinze, *Glass Ceilings*, 66–7.
29 n.a., "Not All Gaps Are Created Equal: The True Value of Care Work," *Oxfam International*, May 25, 2022, https://www.oxfam.org/en/not-all-gaps-are-created-equal-true-value-care-work.
30 "The Missing Piece: Valuing Women's Unrecognized Contribution to the Economy," *UNDP*, https://www.undp.org/latin-america/blog/missing-piece-valuing-womens-unrecognized-contribution-economy (accessed August 27, 2024).
31 Hochschild, "Can Emotional Labor Be Fun?," 30.
32 Michele Saracino, *Christian Anthropology: An Introduction to the Human Person* (New York: Paulist Press, 2015), 50.
33 Mary Doak, *Divine Harmony: Seeking Community in a Broken World* (New York: Paulist Press, 2017), 10.
34 Shane Clifton, *Crippled Grace: Disability, Virtue Ethics, and the Good Life*, Studies in Religion, Theology, and Disability (Waco, TX: Baylor University Press, 2018), 200.
35 Clifton, *Crippled Grace*, 201–2.
36 Hinze, *Glass Ceilings*, 16. Italics in original.
37 Leah Libresco Sargeant, "The Romney Family Plan Sees the True Value of Parenting," *The New York Times*, February 18, 2021, https://www.nytimes.com/2021/02/18/opinion/mitt-romney-family-plan.html.

38 One of the movement's leaders, Silvia Federici, noted that members disagreed about whether "wages for housework" was a serious demand or a way to signal refusal of "housework" labor altogether. Federici and Austin, *The New York Wages for Housework Committee 1972–1977*, 19.
39 Federici and Austin, *The New York Wages for Housework Committee 1972–1977*, 19.
40 Federici and Austin, *The New York Wages for Housework Committee 1972–1977*, 43.
41 Nadasen, *Care*, 16; Mignon Duffy, "Reproductive Labor," in *Sociology of Work: An Encyclopedia*, ed. Vicki Smith (SAGE Reference, 2013), Gale eBooks, ; Tithi Bhattacharya, "Introduction: Mapping Social Reproduction Theory," in *Social Reproduction Theory*, ed. Tithi Bhattacharya, Remapping Class, Recentering Oppression (London: Pluto Press, 2017), 2, https://doi.org/10.2307/j.ctt1vz494j.5. A detailed history of Western feminist thought on reproductive labor and its relationship to productive labor is Susan J. Ferguson, *Women and Work: Feminism, Labour, and Social Reproduction* (Las Vegas, NV: Pluto Press, 2020).
42 Tithi Bhattacharya, ed., "Crisis of Care? On the Social-Reproductive Contradictions of Contemporary Capitalism," in *Social Reproduction Theory: Remapping Class, Recentring Oppression*, ed. Nancy Fraser, Ebook Collection (JSTOR) (Las Vegas, NV: Pluto Press, 2017), 23.
43 "How Much Is a Mother Really Worth?," *Salary.Com* (blog), May 10, 2019, https://www.salary.com/articles/mother-salary/; Zameena Mejia, "These Are the 25 Best-Paying Jobs in America in 2019, According to US News & World Report," *CNBC*, January 10, 2019, https://www.cnbc.com/2019/01/08/the-are-the-25-best-paying-jobs-in-america-in-2019-according-to-us-newsworld-report--.html. 2019 is the last year for which the website published these calculations.
44 n.a., "Not All Gaps Are Created Equal."
45 Stephanie Murray, "Breastfeeding Isn't Free. What If That Work Was Included in the GDP?," *Washington Post*, July 6, 2020, https://www.washingtonpost.com/gender-identity/breastfeeding-isnt-free-what-if-that-work-was-included-in-the-gdp/.
46 Hinze, *Glass Ceilings*.
47 Hinze, *Glass Ceilings*, 88–90.
48 Amber Lapp, "Should a Child Benefit Be Based on Marital and Employment Status?," *American Compass* (blog), May 4, 2021, https://

americancompass.org/the-commons/should-a-child-benefit-be-based-on-marital-and-employment-status/.
49 Petersen, *Can't Even*, 212.
50 Sheryl Sandberg, *Lean In: Women, Work, and the Will to Lead* (New York: Alfred A. Knopf, 2013), 120.
51 Beck, "The Concept Creep of 'Emotional Labor.'"

4

Drudgery and Flow: The Labor of Food

Chapter Outline

Flow: When Work Restores Us	66
Transforming the Goods of Creation	70
Food Work as Livelihood: Sharing the Goods of Creation	73
Solution: Sacramental View of the Goods of Creation	82
Conclusion	87

Like many families in the spring of 2020, mine was hunkered down to avoid contracting or transmitting Covid-19. While we worried and prayed for essential workers and the sick, we struggled with the far more manageable problems of lockdown, including the need to eat. With restaurants closed and our shopping trips kept to a minimum, the daily labor of food prep and cleanup consumed more of my day than I would have thought possible. While my husband cared for our toddler, I taught my classes online, then rushed to the kitchen to see what remained from our last grocery order and figure out how to turn it into dinner. Whether it was the monotonous work or the sameness of my own cooking, after a few months of this, nothing sounded or even tasted good. I had lost my appetite.

Food is identity, nourishment, pleasure, connection—and food is also labor. In fact, the work that brings food to our tables is some of the most challenging and dangerous that Americans do. The highest risks of death on the job are borne, not by police or firefighters, but by farmworkers and fishermen.¹ Hospitality has the highest industry-wide rate of sexual harassment, and most service workers who report their harassment experience some form of (illegal) retaliation.² Retail consistently ranks as the second-highest industry for illnesses and injuries sustained on the job, second only to health care—not surprising, when we remember that grocery store workers were deemed "essential" and required to work even at the height of the Covid-19 pandemic.³ And many food workers are excluded from US labor law protections. Farmworkers and restaurant servers can legally be paid less than minimum wage, and owners of small farms have effectively no legal accountability when workers there are injured or even killed on the job.⁴ These hardships for workers persist despite food's obvious importance to human life and to local and national economies. Fully ten percent of US jobs are in agriculture, restaurants, or other food-related industries, and worldwide, about one in seven people work in food.⁵

Food is labor at home, too. Not all of us will work in restaurants, groceries or fields, but every adult has made a sandwich or an iced coffee and engaged in the labor of sustaining themselves through food. The last chapter discussed reproductive labor, which reproduces the worker's body and energy and the communities where we live our lives. Food preparation and cleanup are a key example of reproductive labor, which must be repeated daily to achieve its purpose. Across the population, at-home food labor remains deeply unequal by gender, with women performing fifty daily minutes of cooking work on average, and men only twenty.⁶ (The labor of food shopping, meal planning, keeping track of what needs to be bought and family dietary needs and preferences, and of course, cleaning up was not counted in this study. As cooks know, each of those tasks contributes significantly to the workload of food preparation.) In male-female couples, cooking, groceries, and cleanup are most often women's primary responsibility, even when both partners work full-time.⁷ Unsurprisingly, household chore responsibilities are one of the most common reasons couples fight; in male-female couples, it's usually women who are most unhappy with the status quo.⁸ A cross-national study of labor data found that "the greater a woman's economic choices, the less time she spends cooking and doing dishes."⁹ As this suggests, avoiding food prep work usually means outsourcing it to someone in greater economic need; it does not guarantee that the work done will be fairly paid nor that the work remaining will be fairly divided by gender.

It's also true that despite the real challenges of this work and persistent inequalities in its practice, many people find satisfaction and purpose in at-home food preparation. Few of us can afford to outsource all the labor that goes into sourcing and preparing what we eat. As food is so intimately bound up with how we pursue health, express our culture, exercise creativity, and care for ourselves and others, I venture to say that many of us would not want to, either.

As 2020 dragged on, Milwaukee activists joined the nationwide movement of protest against racist police brutality, marching and demonstrating in support of Black Lives Matter. A group of neighbors organized to provide the marchers with bottled water, sign materials, and other supplies, and I volunteered to cook this group dinner. Still avoiding extra trips to the store, I raided our pantry and freezer and even baked bread for the sandwiches.[10] I spent a long day in the kitchen, playing music and smudging up my phone as I searched for recipes. My back ached, my feet hurt, and every pan I owned was dirty. So why, I thought with surprise as I dropped the food off, did I feel so content?

When we recognize, with Catholic social teaching, that unpaid work is work, we confront what seems to be a paradox: unpaid work can feel deeply enjoyable, even energizing us—and this can be true even when we're already tired from work. After a long day at your paid job, sometimes cooking a new recipe or tackling a home project can leave you feeling not depleted, but restored. For cookbook author Deb Perelman, this is a selling point about food work: "I didn't want a book whose goal was to rush you out of the kitchen the second you began to unwind. I didn't want to operate from the assumption that cooking is drudgery, when for so many of us, it's a much-needed escape."[11] As Perelman hints, for many of us, cooking is a way into one of the experiences that can make work so rewarding: the immersive, restorative experience psychologist Mihaly Csikszentmihalyi calls flow. Growing and even harvesting food (apple-picking, anyone?) are other examples of food work that many people find so deeply rewarding and even flow-inducing that we do them without pay, simply for the pleasure of working toward a goal.

This chapter uses food work as a lens to continue exploring work in Catholic social teaching. First, the examples above invite us to think about flow and other ways work can restore us. The lens of food work offers insight into Catholic social teaching's understanding of work as transforming the materials of creation. We'll explore how Catholic and other thinkers connect this aspect of work to its ability to restore us. We examine Catholic thought on agricultural work, which recommends aggressive government intervention in particular cases of farmworker exploitation, and contrast the tradition's uncompromising vision of worker justice with the reality of paid food labor in the United States. We reflect on historical reasons why a sadly common thread in paid food work is precarity, poor treatment, and low pay. Finally, I propose that a sacramental understanding of the materials of creation can help us see the benefits of work in our lives, through the example of unpaid food work, and remind us to hunger for justice for those whose paid food work earns their daily bread.

Flow: When Work Restores Us

Perelman's image of a cook finally "unwinding" in the kitchen after a long day of other pursuits points us toward how good it can feel to become absorbed in a challenging task. Psychologist Mihaly Csikszentmihalyi observed that when we are invested in a task that is complex enough to demand our full attention, we experience a positive feeling of being carried along by an energy internal to the process.[12] He calls this positive, fully engaged state *flow*. In flow, "people become so involved in what they are doing that the activity becomes spontaneous, almost automatic; they stop becoming aware of themselves as separate from the actions they are performing."[13] We achieve flow most easily during activities that challenge our skills and direct our actions toward goals, as well as tasks where feedback is built into the process and where control is possible although not guaranteed.[14] Think about sports, games, or the arts, where we pursue a certain goal and develop skills toward mastery, but without the guarantee we will succeed. And clearly, the possibility of achieving flow is not limited to paid employment. We've been discussing examples of flow experienced by home cooks, and Csikszentmihalyi uses the possibility of deep engagement in caring for children as another example.[15]

Csikszentmihalyi became interested in flow when researching ways to motivate workers by helping them enjoy their jobs. Indeed, paid work is a common way many of us experience a flow state.[16] In a time use study, both manual and knowledge workers reported they were in flow twice as often on the job, in a study where researchers contacted them randomly throughout the day, than in their time outside work. Yet when asked, the people in the study said they preferred other pastimes to work, even though the positive flow state seemed to be more accessible at work than elsewhere.[17] Csikszentmihalyi concludes that "when it comes to work, people do not heed the evidence of their senses. They disregard the quality of immediate experience, and base their motivation instead on the strongly rooted cultural stereotype of what work is *supposed* to be like."[18] That is, we expect work to be unpleasant, even though for many of us it provides the structure, goals, and challenges that make flow possible. We may expect all leisure activities to be more enjoyable than work, even though passive activities like watching TV or consuming social media are less likely to induce flow compared to more engaging and challenging activities like playing sports, working on home projects, or cooking.

The high likelihood of achieving flow at work is strong evidence in favor of Catholic social teaching's view that work is an important key to a meaningful life. In fact, it is precisely because some activities are work that they induce flow. Flow can occur where a task's level of challenge meets our level of skill; this means that we have to be attempting to do or change something in the world, activities CST would consider work. The vaguely dissatisfied feeling we get after binge-watching TV or endlessly scrolling social media means, among other things, that the activity does not challenge us or allow us to develop our skills. As Csikszentmihalyi suggests, we anticipate wrongly what will fulfill us and restore us when we expect our recreation time to be passive, devoid of challenge, and not to include any tasks that could be described as work. When John Paul II describes the sense of purpose and pride that can be found in work, he is describing not just the reward of on-the-job achievements, but the sense of relaxation and renewal Deb Perelman finds in her home kitchen. "Enjoyment depends on increasing complexity,"[19] Csikszentmihalyi observed, and the reproductive labor of food preparation offers us a chance to experience creativity as we try new ingredients and skills.

Novel items or techniques are a reliable draw for food manufacturers, who understand how compelling tackling a new challenge can be to those who seek flow through food preparation. When sales of convenient boxed cake mixes slowed in the 1950s, a marketing expert revived them by emphasizing the creativity bakers could exercise in decorating their cakes with frosting.[20] Today, creators on TikTok and YouTube introduce many home cooks to new skills, ingredients, or techniques. Certainly, cooking is not the only way to access flow through unpaid work, but considering that most of us have access to the materials and all of us need to eat, it might be the most accessible way to reliably experience flow at home.[21]

Another detailed explanation of how flow-inducing work can restore us comes from a widely popular book on burnout by two educators (who are also twin sisters), Amelia Nagoski and Emily Nagoski. When we experience stress—whether from real physical threats or more ordinary stress in the workplace or in daily life—our bodies flood with neurotransmitters that help us fight, flee, or freeze. These responses would help us if the threat demanded a physical response, but they can harm the body over time if the stress response becomes chronic.[22] The Nagoskis suggest that burnout is what happens when we don't "complete the stress cycle," which means signaling to our bodies that the threat is gone and we are safe.[23] We can complete the stress cycle and signal to our embodied selves that safety is here through many familiar tactics, including positive social interaction, deep breathing, or getting a hug. I was fascinated to learn that some methods science recommends to complete the stress cycle—dealing with the stress and burnout that can come from paid employment—involve activities that Catholic social teaching also considers work.

"*Physical activity is the single most efficient activity for completing the stress cycle*," the Nagoskis write, in italics. "Physical activity is what tells your brain you have successfully survived the threat and now your body is a safe place to live."[24] Furthermore, creative activity can help us complete the stress cycle and even predict feelings of well-being the following day.[25] Exercise would certainly be considered work by Catholic social teaching, but most forms of household labor are physical activity even if we don't usually think of them as exercise—and some are creative, as well. Whether or not she realizes it, the worker unwinding in her kitchen at home, exercising creativity and using her body to achieve something good, has tapped into a science-backed method for protecting herself from burnout due to work stress.

To be clear, the Nagoskis' research on the stress cycle does not advocate dealing with work-related anxiety by devoting more and more time to the job that stresses us out in the first place, common though this is as a way to cope. Stress at work can lead to burnout, often because of concerns related to working conditions, such as overwork or bias: we burn out when struggling to carry something we should not have to handle. Their aim is not to help us deal with work stress so we can continue to absorb more of it, becoming more efficient paid employees. Rather, they want to empower people to "deal with the stress so you can deal with the stressor."[26] When people feel well enough to move beyond the feeling of being "stuck" in the stress response, they can evaluate what about their work life needs to change.[27]

Is this paradoxical—that we can unwind stress from work by engaging in, well, more work? After all, physical and creative activities are still work for Catholic social teaching.

But the Nagoskis' findings that work can help us complete the stress cycle, restoring our bodies to healthy equilibrium, confirm the tradition's insight that work is a good thing for human beings. Many of us have had the experience of burning off the stress of a long day with a workout, sinking into the experience of cooking dinner, or leaving job worries behind in the chaos of kids' bedtime. While work can stress us out, engaging in embodied, creative activity can also tell us that we are safe and in the right place—an example of a time when work, in this case unpaid work, is indeed a good thing for us.

Many stressed-out workers understandably conclude that they must cope by engaging in less unpaid labor—so cooking, chores, and volunteering get outsourced or dropped, replaced with a screen-saturated downtime that's as passive as possible. But Catholic social teaching and the science the Nagoskis consult suggest that this understandable response might be misguided. Instead, spending time baking, volunteering, or taking care of projects around the house might be just the thing our bodies need to complete the stress cycle. This doesn't mean that unjust conditions leading to burnout at work or inequalities in unpaid labor at home are OK or should be justified. But it confirms the insight of Catholic social teaching that work, not just paid work, can be good for us. Then, if work is harmful, like the work that leads to burnout, we know that this is not inherent to what work is, but something wrong with the working conditions—which we can advocate to change.

Transforming the Goods of Creation

Many authors have pointed out that skilled manual labor—working with our hands on tasks that also engage our minds—seems especially well suited to elicit the positive experience of flow. For these authors, working with physical materials delivers the engaging challenge, built-in feedback, and goal direction that set us up for an enjoyable flow experience. This may be especially true when our work deals with natural materials, with their inherent variation, although manufactured materials can challenge workers too. The insights of thinkers who reflect on manual labor echo the way Catholic social teaching envisions humans "subduing the earth," a Biblical phrase that means transforming what comes from the earth to make it more useful to us (*LE* 5). This is not just a way of linking modern work to the Biblical creation story, but an important insight into what work is and why it's good for us. Work brings our mental and physical abilities to bear on something that exists outside us, something that has its own internal logic that we can come to understand. This has everything to do with what makes work engaging, challenging, and good for our human nature.

Catholics believe God created all the good things of the earth for humans to enjoy, but observe that we only enjoy them as the result of human work. Human beings "take over ownership of small parts of the various riches of nature: those beneath the ground, those in the sea, on land, or in space . . . through work and for work" (*LE* 12). Everything that contributes to creating wealth, from human ideas and labor to the technology we use, ultimately comes from the materials of the natural world transformed through human work. When we are working, we are always working on the material of creation that we "find" and did not create ourselves, and these materials also provide the energy that sustains our bodies in order to do that work (*LE* 12). Whether we're turning vegetables into dinner or determining the load-bearing capacities of steel alloys, at some point our work must answer to an outside authority: the properties of the material we received from nature and did not create ourselves. This builds many good things into our work: a reminder to be humble, a connection to nature, and an opportunity to experience flow by pursuing an activity that challenges us. Our work develops our own abilities to understand and use nature's materials, confirming our role as the creatures who do the task God gave to us alone: to use our reason and bodies to put the earth's gifts to use. By doing this, we develop ourselves, we who are also part of creation (*LE* 6).

The insight that the goods of creation challenge us by requiring our work to meet their own internal standard is clearly present in Catholic social teaching, but I understood it first by reading philosophers who think about manual labor. Rebecca May Johnson, a philosopher of food and cooking, wrote about how turning ingredients into food brings her into contact with a reality outside herself:

> I have a revelation about ingredients, or vegetables: they are *things*. I must learn to watch them closely, ready to accommodate their whims, which are not human. The recipe is a method for responding to things. . . . When I perform the recipe, things become other things in a mess[y] transformation. . . . They spatter my shirt red.[28]

Johnson suggests that the cook's skill lies in paying attention to the properties of her ingredients, which are governed by their own rules, which she must observe and learn to follow. Matthew Crawford, a philosopher and motorcycle mechanic, finds similar insights in his meditation on manual labor. "Skilled manual labor entails a systematic encounter with the material world," he writes, "precisely the kind of encounter that gives rise to natural science . . . . Through pragmatic engagement, the carpenter learns the different species of wood, their fitness for such needs as load bearing and water holding, their dimensional stability with changes in the weather, and their varying resistance to rot and insects."[29]

Through reflective work, mechanics, carpenters, or cooks acquire an understanding of the properties of their materials and are able to turn that understanding to solve problems. Crawford explains through this example:

> A sheared-off pin has blocked an oil gallery, resulting in oil starvation to the head [of a motorcycle's engine]. . . . This is the Truth, and it is the same for everyone. But finding this truth requires a certain disposition in the individual: attentiveness, enlivened by a sense of responsibility to the motorcycle. . . . The truth does not reveal itself to idle spectators.[30]

Thus, manual labor is not simply manual but demands a sustained practice of attention, involving the exercise of the intellect and the virtues. Similarly,

Johnson explains that in cooking, we integrate intellectual knowledge with our own practical, embodied understanding of how things work: "Even when I cook without looking at a recipe on a page, I am always referring to an index of recipes in which I, we, are always immersed. Any 'new' dish I make is a composite of fragments I have seen, eaten, heard about in passing and which I repeat in a new constellation."[31]

Johnson and Crawford seem to suggest that skilled manual labor demands engagement with reality in a way that, we might think, intellectual labor does not. But for Catholic social teaching, work does not have to be manual to place us in that relationship with reality that both philosophers find so beneficial. Working with words, bytes, laws, or digital images can provide that combination of challenge and external standard that makes our work meaningful to us and to the society that needs it—and rewards us by connecting us to flow. For Catholic social teaching, "the biblical words 'subdue the earth' . . . undoubtedly include also *a relationship with technology,* with the world of machinery which is the fruit of the work of the human intellect and a historical confirmation of [human] dominion over nature" (*LE* 5).

In other words, the materials of creation are still God's gifts even after humans transform them into books, semiconductors, or other tools for intellectual work. Sitting at a desk forming words into effective communication demands expertise in human language and the social contexts nuancing each word's connotation. Designing a building or making calculations in a spreadsheet demands knowledge of technologies that the worker did not create, but which she must understand and respect for her work to be effective in shaping the world. Work in which we learn about and act out of our understanding of creation's predictable properties—and in doing so, challenge ourselves and develop our abilities—does not have to be manual labor.

Recently, the Catholic social teaching tradition has worked to correct misunderstandings of the biblical command to "subdue the earth." In the past, this was misinterpreted to mean that humans could do whatever we wanted with the gifts of creation, exploiting nature and nonhuman creatures with no thought to sustainability. As Pope Francis writes, the biblical creation story really envisions "a relationship of mutual responsibility between human beings and nature" (*LS'* 67). We can understand this better when we see how working with the gifts of creation transforms us as persons. Not only do the plants, minerals, and animals we work with enrich our lives by meeting our human needs, but learning to adjust our way of working to the internal logic of these materials of creation shapes our own knowledge and skills. The many ways we benefit from the materials of creation underscore the importance of using our human reason to steward natural resources wisely.

To say that work responds to the real properties of creation is not to say that any work *necessarily* changes us for the better. (As a lurid example, the work of the executioner or "hit man" deals with the knowledge of the human body's need for oxygen, tolerance for electricity, or capacity for blood loss. Catholic social teaching would view such work as deeply, spiritually harmful to the worker as well as to the community.) It is simply to describe what we are doing when we are working—responding to the real characteristics of creation—and how this helps explain how work shapes us. We are always working on the materials of creation when we work, even if we're sitting at a computer. But skilled manual labor, including cooking and other food work, can help us better understand what work means for us as humans through the reminder of how it feels to transform the materials of creation directly, using our bodily senses and gaining new understanding in the process.

Food Work as Livelihood: Sharing the Goods of Creation

So far, we've been talking about food work as we do it at home, the daily reproductive labor that helps sustain our own bodies and the bodies of those we care for. But of course, for many people—about 10 percent of the US working population, and around one in seven worldwide—food work is how we earn a living, too. It is obvious that no one could survive without farmers, processors, and other food workers, and yet in many societies this work is unnecessarily precarious, dangerous, and underpaid. For Catholic social teaching, societies should recognize the immense importance of food work by ensuring dignity and a just living for these workers, even if this requires drastic changes to a community's laws and practices.

The Catholic social teaching tradition has always stressed the importance of agricultural work to people who do it and the communities that rely on what they produce. Uneasy with the changes to working conditions and social life that the Industrial Revolution ushered in, Pope Leo XIII envisioned self-supporting family farms as the model for work that provided dignity, security, and a balance between work and family life (*RN* 5, 47). While farms are important to those who work them, the tradition consistently points out that they are important to all of us: by nourishing our bodies, agriculture becomes the basis for all other productive human activity (*LE* 5). Agriculture reminds us what work is: a practice of transforming the goods of creation, through which we transform ourselves (*LE* 9). However, the tradition acknowledges that despite its importance, farm work is often under-respected and mistreated:

> The world of agriculture, which provides society with the goods it needs for its daily sustenance, is of *fundamental importance*. . . . Agricultural work involves considerable difficulties, including unremitting and sometimes exhausting physical effort and a lack of appreciation on the part of society. . . . In many situations radical and urgent changes are therefore needed in order to restore to agriculture—and to rural people—their just value *as the basis for a healthy economy,* within the social community's development as a whole. (*LE* 21)

The disconnect between the importance of farmwork and its low status in many communities leads the Catholic social tradition to a remarkable place: the *only* time the tradition calls for expropriation—government seizure of private property—is in a particular situation of injustice to farmworkers. Before we talk about this situation, called *latifundia*, we need a quick introduction to the tradition's teaching on private property. A key insight of Catholic social teaching is the universal destination of goods, the understanding that "God intended the earth with everything contained in it for the use of all human beings" (*GS* 69). The implications of this view can be challenging, because it means that the right to private property does not outweigh every human's right to the basic goods they need to live. Since the time of the first Christians, Catholic tradition has consistently said that if you have a surplus—more than you need to live—while others lack their basic needs, those needy people have a right to the property that makes up your surplus. If you own more than you need while poverty exists, the poor have more of a right to your excess than you do.

Chaos! Anarchy! Communism! Well—not exactly. The tradition isn't advocating we break into luxury homes to redistribute wealth, or rob grocery stores to feed the hungry. Instead, the universal destination of goods challenges everyone, from policymakers to ordinary income earners, to distribute the goods of the earth so that all can have their needs met—think private charity and progressive tax rates, not search and seizure. Similarly, the dignity of work includes a right to work for those who need to, but generally, the Catholic tradition does not prescribe a specific way for people to access their right to work. Instead of suggesting that the government employ everyone who needs work, for example, CST documents typically suggest that governments, business, and labor should collaborate to ensure that dignified work at family-supporting wages is available for all who need it.[32] However, there is one instance where Catholic social teaching explicitly calls on the government to seize property from the wealthy in order to distribute it to the poor, as a specific path to ensuring the right to work. It indicates just how important food-producing labor is in Catholic social teaching, because of its importance to all human beings. This is the teaching on what are called *latifundia*.

Latifundia is a Latin term used for large properties of land in Central and South America, where Catholic communities first became concerned about a particular way wealthy landowners were misusing their large properties.[33] (CST uses *latifundia* to refer to specific misuses of farmable land that come about because of wealth concentration, when small farmers can no longer afford to keep their farmland and must sell it to wealthy property owners. When small farmers lose the right to work on lands their families have historically tended, or when farmable land is wasted through use for something other than crops, CST judges that land is wrongly being treated as an investment, violating its primary purpose, which is to provide food. There is no English term that captures both the size of the property and the patterns of misuse, so I'm sticking with the Latin here.)

The term dates back to the Roman Empire, where *latifundia* were large landed estates worked by enslaved people. In many ways, workers on contemporary *latifundia* are not much better off. For example, in twentieth-century El Salvador, wealthy investors growing crops like coffee for export steadily bought up the land of smaller farmers who couldn't pay their mortgages. These farmers ended up stuck working the land they had previously owned while taking home less of their own proceeds because they now had a landlord to pay.[34] In many Central and South American countries, *latifundia* are used to grow crops for export or in some cases, left uncultivated as investment properties while people in nearby communities go hungry.

Historically, the United States had a practice similar to *latifundia*: sharecropping. In the southern United States after Emancipation, the law supported former slaveowners who imposed exploitative conditions on freed people who worked the land. "Planters used the hunger of the formerly enslaved people as a means of regaining control over their labor," writes historian Jennifer Jensen Wallach.[35] With no legal title to the land their families had worked for generations, many African American freed people and their descendants entered into exploitative sharecropping contracts that left them dependent on landowners for their own meager food supply, even while their work produced valuable cash crops.[36] The position of sharecroppers, "the primary form of labor organization on southern [US] farms until the 1940s," is similar to those who farm *latifundia* in Central and South America. The hard, skilled, and socially crucial labor of these farmworkers does not afford them a decent living, a path out of poverty, or any hope of purchasing their own land.[37] While those working there suffered hunger and malnutrition, sharecropped farms grew food for sale far away. In the same way, *latifundia* are used for export crops or, worse, treated as investment properties and not farmed at all.

This brings us back to the universal destination of goods. The Catholic social tradition criticizes *latifundia*, but not just because they came about through injustice or because workers suffer there. Rather, the use of *latifundia* to enrich the wealthy in a world where hunger persists and farmers are willing to work is an injustice to a whole society in need of a reliable food supply. This is why, in the case of *latifundia*—and only in this case—Catholic social teaching explicitly calls for expropriation, where the government takes private property or changes the laws that allow property to be privately owned in order to secure a public benefit.[38] This teaching was first laid out by Vatican Council II, which wrote in *Gaudium et Spes*:

> In many underdeveloped regions there are large or even extensive rural estates which are only slightly cultivated or lie completely idle for the sake of profit, while the majority of the people either are without land or have only very small fields. . . . Not infrequently those who are hired to work for the landowners or who till a portion of the land as tenants receive a wage or income unworthy of a human being, lack decent housing and are exploited by middlemen. Deprived of all security, they live under such

personal servitude that almost every opportunity of acting on their own initiative and responsibility is denied to them. . . . Indeed, *insufficiently cultivated estates should be distributed to those who can make these lands fruitful*. (*GS* 71, my italics)

Popes Paul VI and John Paul II both repeated the call for expropriation in their own encyclicals, stressing unjust working conditions and calling for land to belong to those who will manage it well.[39] Pope Francis, too, was critical of those who use the legal system to confiscate land from those who historically farmed it.[40]

The Pontifical Council for Justice and Peace observed that the existence of *latifundia* is not a coincidence, but intentional "misappropriation of land by large landholders or national or international companies, at times with the support of State institutions."[41] Concentrated ownership of land impoverishes farm families, tramples on the rights of Indigenous communities, and irreversibly harms the environment.[42] The final goal of expropriation is not for the government to own the land, but for it to return to, and remain the property of, relatively small farmers who will grow food for the local community.[43] The tradition consistently finds that when land is not being used in a way that serves all of society, expropriation is justified, "with adequate compensation to the owners," so land can be returned to those who will farm it for the benefit of everyone.[44]

The fact that *latifundia* is the only instance where Catholic social teaching openly recommends expropriation is not because those farmers suffer more than impoverished workers elsewhere, or because the process that creates *latifundia* is more unjust than other instances of wealth inequality. Rather, it points to the crucial purpose of land worked by humans: to provide food for the whole community. In the Catholic understanding, land is not simply property for the owner to use or waste as they please. As the source of life-sustaining food, it is a gift from God to all members of society, and for farmers, it is the "means of production," the necessary ingredient for important and dignified work. If it were common for wealthy investors to buy up work tools and keep them to rust while workers needed them, I believe Catholic social teaching might call for expropriation in that case, too. For now, it is only in the case of landhoarding that Catholic social teaching calls on governments—with all the power of their criminal justice systems and standing armies—to take private property away from owners, in order to put it to a better use.

Returning *latifundia* to those who will farm the land not only benefits those farmers but also enriches the whole society they serve by ensuring plentiful, secure food production. Catholic social teaching's call for expropriation is a strong reminder that the work farmworkers do is necessary for the survival of all of society.

Expropriation has not been proposed as a solution to injustice in the agricultural and food industries in the United States, where farmland going unused is not a significant problem. However, there is a similar reality of concentration of farmable land among fewer large property owners, giving them outsize power to exploit workers. The US bishops consistently urge stronger support for small family farms in their advocacy around the yearly "farm bill," which distributes federal funds to the agriculture industry. This reality, and the legal landscape that excludes farmworkers from many protections, places US farmworkers in situations of similar precarity to those who work on *latifundia*, "break[ing] their backs in serf-like conditions for disgracefully low wages," as the bishops wrote.[45]

If food work is so important to the functioning of human societies, why have so many of them—including some of the wealthiest nations—deliberately created structures that endanger the lives and livelihoods of workers who do it? "Workers in America's agricultural fields are regularly subjected to abuses ranging from high occurrences of sexual assault and harassment, wage theft and safety issues including injuries, fatalities on the job and exposure to hazardous chemicals," summarizes a reporter for *The Guardian*.[46] Even when laws do protect farmworkers, poor enforcement means employers are unlikely to experience any consequences for mistreating them. "Small farms exemptions" in laws about worker safety and workplace compensation mean farm employers with small staffs bear virtually no legal responsibility when their workers are injured or even killed on the job.[47] Due to this lack of meaningful oversight, agriculture ranks among the industries with the highest rates of death at work (along with forestry and another food provision job, fishing).[48] Only a few states offer farmworkers the guarantee most US workers have of a legally protected framework for forming a union.[49] And farmworkers who are undocumented may fear retaliation and even deportation, which keeps them from turning to the legal system to protect their rights in the case of underpayment, abuse, or even sexual assault.[50]

The work of processing, preparing, and serving food carries similar injustices. Slaughterhouse work, "considered morally and physically repellent by the vast majority of society," carries social stigma, harms workers' mental health, and exposes workers to repetitive stress injuries and dangerous cuts, as well as the loss of limbs.[51] Similarly, processing seafood is detailed, repetitive manual labor. Under long hours with few accommodations, workers can develop repetitive strain injuries to their hands, back and neck as well as the risk of infected cuts.[52] Both industries, like agriculture, frequently hire undocumented workers who may feel less able to stand up for their rights for fear of deportation. Even restaurant work is not immune from labor mistreatment. In many states, tipped workers can legally be paid below minimum wage, with seventeen states allowing these food workers to earn as little as $2.13 an hour.[53] A "customer is always right" mentality coupled with low wages can lead to the expectation for service workers to absorb any abuse customers dish out. When journalist Emily Guendelsberger worked at McDonald's, she asked her coworkers what items customers had thrown at them after enduring her own attack. "The list encompasses pretty much everything in the store," she wrote, including hot coffee, full cups of soda, and ice cream cones.[54]

In addition to underpaying and mistreating food workers, our society seems to expect their labor to be invisible. Political scientist Timothy Pachirat, who worked undercover at a slaughterhouse, describes this work as "hidden in plain sight."[55] When journalist Tracie McMillan worked undercover as a farm laborer in California, she spoke of constantly driving around and getting lost, indicating how hard it was to observe farm laborers at work even when she had been told where to go and was actively looking for them.[56] Food is a source of health, pleasure, and connection, but US eaters seem to want the labor that brings it to us cheap, exploitable, and concealed, so we don't even have to think about workers' injustices. Why are some of the worst, most dangerous jobs in food?

As with *latifundia*, the poor working conditions for US food workers are permitted and upheld by laws passed by our government, laws influenced by social biases about which groups of workers can be treated as disposable. Farmworkers are not protected by the National Labor Relations Act, which granted many protections to workers in most industries. When the Act was passed in 1935, most farm labor was done by African American descendants of enslaved workers. The law's framers believed excluding farmworkers from labor protections was necessary for their law to pass in an era of open racism.[57] Throughout the twentieth century, the United States also came to rely on migrant workers, including many from Mexico and Latin America, for crucial farm labor.[58] Both their transient status and the fear of deportation for non-citizen workers make these workers vulnerable. Slaughterhouse work is another example of highly valuable, deeply stigmatized food labor which has passed from marginalized group to marginalized group. Once primarily European immigrants in the era of Upton Sinclair's *The Jungle*, slaughterhouse workers today are primarily African American or Latin American migrant workers. Reliance on undocumented workers, who are less likely to challenge mistreatment for fear of deportation, is an endemic practice. State governments have passed "ag-gag" laws, supported by the food processing industry, which make it a crime to record or share information about what takes place inside slaughterhouses, with an obvious chilling effect for workers taking action to improve their conditions.

Even while our laws grant food workers fewer rights than workers in other professions, the US government has taken action to keep food prices low, often at a cost to the workers who bring it to us.[59] Recently, during the Covid-19 pandemic, meatpacking industry groups stoked fears of shortages to convince the federal government to declare slaughterhouse employees "essential workers," with the predictable outcome of disproportionate Covid deaths among this vulnerable group.[60] Laws and policies prioritizing the availability of food over the dignity and safety of the workers who produce it treat food like a commodity, not what it is—a gift of God's creation, brought to each of us via difficult, skilled human labor.

As we can see, some of the poor conditions and compensation for food workers are determined directly by employers, but government policies and real or perceived consumer demand also play a role. Catholic social teaching has tools to describe these different sources of responsibility for workers. The "direct employer" is the person or company we'd traditionally think of as a worker's employer, who hires them and sets the terms of their work. However, the "indirect employer" also bears significant responsibility for working conditions and wages. Indirect employers affect workers' experience when they shape employment conditions (*LE* 17). For example, governments are often indirect employers when they set trade policies, regulate worker safety and hours, or establish minimum wage laws (*LE*

17). International organizations, nonprofits, and labor unions also play a role in shaping the conditions of labor markets that affect direct employers as they set working conditions and wages for their employees.

When we choose to boycott products made in unjust conditions or companies that support causes we disagree with, or when we make an effort to support local or worker-owned businesses, we may see ourselves as the "indirect employer" of the workers who make what we buy. We want to use our purchasing power to support good working conditions instead of rewarding employers who profit from injustice. Scholars who study Catholic social teaching debate whether it makes sense to see individual consumers as "indirect employers" in this way. Albino Barrera, an economist and theologian, says that particularly in today's globalized economy, "we have truly become each other's indirect employers because we are in effect consumers of each other's work effort and output."[61] Others argue that since people need to purchase so many different things and each individual product is part of complicated supply chains, it is unrealistic to view individual consumers as even indirectly responsible for the workers who produce the things we buy.[62] It is also true that even if we view consumers as indirect employers, not everyone can afford to make different choices. My neighborhood Facebook group regularly breaks out in debate between those who advocate supporting local farms or shopping at our neighborhood co-op, and others who cannot afford the higher costs of food that comes to us under more ethical conditions.

Some people go to great lengths to ensure their food is produced under conditions that are as fair as possible for workers, but this is not possible for many consumers, and we all need to eat. I believe Catholic social teaching would urge us to focus on the responsibility of indirect employers in the many injustices we see in the food industry. *Latifundia* in Latin America, sharecropping in the US's recent past, and poor wages and conditions for present-day US food workers are creations of the legal landscape, whether openly permitted by law or enabled by weak enforcement. To bring about justice for the people who bring food to our tables, taking action to change the legal landscape seems more effective than altering individual purchasing choices. Of course, governments should work to ensure that people can access enough food easily and reliably; any other right that we have depends on our bodies' survival. But ensuring food security for a whole population should not come at the expense of safety, dignity, and fair pay for food workers.

The labor organization United Farm Workers gained national attention in the 1970s by urging consumer boycotts that helped them win union contracts with individual farming companies. More recently, they have used their lobbying power to advance laws protecting all farmworkers at the federal and state levels, with notable successes in California and New York.[63] Similarly, the Coalition of Immokalee Workers broadened its focus from fighting for better wages across Florida's tomato industry to pressuring international brands to agree to fair farmworker wages throughout their supply chains.[64] Food is personal and cultural, but it is also affected by the choices of governments and international businesses. Focusing on these indirect employers can be an effective way to reverse the historical conditions that make food work some of the worst jobs in a given community.

Solution: Sacramental View of the Goods of Creation

Intimately, daily sustaining our bodies and the bodies we care for, food is always personal. Demanding too much complex labor for any one household, food is always necessarily communal. Problems with the way food work gets done range from burnout and gender inequality at home to dangerous conditions and poor wages for paid food workers. Envisioning a more wise and humane approach to the labor of food means we need to think about personal and systemic solutions that acknowledge what food, and food labor, means to us. While some suggest outsourcing food work or leaning into it, neither approach adequately responds to the human dignity of paid and unpaid food workers from farm to factory, grocery store to table.

In response to the challenges of food work at home—which can arise from unequal division of labor or just from the overwhelming amount of work to be done—proposed solutions vary wildly. Women struggling with expectations to do most of the reproductive labor at home are often advised to "outsource it"; order takeout and hire a housecleaner. In her delightful polemic *The Case for Processed Food*, Anastacia Marx de Salcedo argues that equalizing the time women and men spend preparing food—

either by men doing more or by families having more recourse to processed foods—could unleash a wave of women's involvement in paid work, community organizations, and political leadership that the world gravely needs.[65] Socialists even envision "community kitchens" where workers could pick up hot meals on the way home from a paid job.[66] For the purposes of Catholic social teaching, there is nothing wrong with outsourcing food labor to a processor or a restaurant chef, but we would want to ensure that their labor—as for all workers—is safe, just, and fairly compensated.

That said, it will always be the case, for those of us who work paid jobs, that we will leave work and go home to do more work: not all of the labor of caring for ourselves and our dependents, if we have them, can be outsourced. Clearly, equality is urgently needed, both out of fairness to those who do disproportionate food labor, and to ensure that their other family members have the chance to access the flow and satisfaction that home food labor can offer. As I've argued in this chapter, integrated into a just environment for paid and unpaid work, the work we do at home can be good for us. If workers outsource their food and other care labor in order to spend more hours at their paid job, they may miss out on the chance to engage in creative activity that completes the physical stress cycle, as well as meaningful time spent with friends or family.

On the flip side of calls to outsource food labor are voices urging us to lean in, suggesting that we can learn to appreciate food and farmworkers by cooking more in our own kitchens or immersing ourselves in complex cooking projects. For example, popular writers like Michael Pollan and Mark Bittman argue that we would have healthier bodies and relationships if more people cooked and ate at home, especially family dinner. Prophets of the flow-inducing abilities of food labor, they have also earned deserved critique from feminists for over-romanticizing historical household labor and glossing over gender inequities today. Similarly, theologian William Cavanaugh suggests that we practice making things we need, such as bread or music, to appreciate the labor that goes into the objects we consume.[67] Another Christian proponent of "leaning in" to home food work might be Catholic Worker founder Dorothy Day, who believed manual labor was a "spiritual weapon" that helped Christians combat selfishness and pride.[68]

While I agree it can be eye-opening to experience with one's own body the amount of work that goes into making bread or garments, these time-consuming practices are not realistic for everyone, and it isn't necessary to become a proficient baker to understand the dignity of reproductive labor. What is needed is not *more* food work, or avoiding the shortcuts we already have, but a changed attitude toward this work, which may start with understanding how it can help us connect to flow and complete the stress cycle. As Deb Perelman wrote, "I feel staunchly that one way we can make cooking feel like more than just a list of endless tasks to complete, even though it's definitely often that . . . is to focus on how it feels to make something that tastes, smells, and feels phenomenal."[69] Writer Mike Powell found a similar insight at the other end of the process of at-home food work: "Washing dishes by hand, I give myself the chance to remember that . . . most of life is ordinary; that ordinary isn't the enemy but instead something nourishing and unavoidable. . . . Washing up isn't the shouldering of a burden but a renewal of the conditions by which all this—the talking, the eating, the communion—can happen again."[70]

Along with justly distributing the labor of unpaid food work and appreciating its flow-inducing potential, we can better value and respect paid food work by seeing the food we consume not just as a commodity but as the product of labor. Home cooks find it easy to think about the food they make this way. Addison Del Mastro writes, "It's an art and a joy, really, to transform raw ingredients into *food*, to present—to *offer* . . . one's labor and its result, and everything it contains."[71] Del Mastro eloquently captures how something as simple as a meal can simultaneously be itself and stand for something larger: the labor that produced it. This way of understanding a thing as mediating, or bringing to us, a larger reality can be called *sacramental*.

In the Catholic understanding of sacraments, material goods remain themselves while containing and communicating a reality that goes beyond them. For example, in the Mass, bread and wine become the sacrament of the Eucharist, pointing beyond themselves to the reality of God's love for humanity. In the words of theologian Susan Ross, "The symbol bears within itself what it communicates; it is not a mere vessel for an extrinsic message."[72] Ordinary food is not a sacrament, but it is sacramental: it makes present and visible the labor that went into transforming ingredients into something good to eat. A sandwich, sweater, or smartphone is not simply a commodity to purchase or even a symbol for hours of skilled or drudge-filled human labor; it is the product and physical manifestation of those hours of work. A sacramental attitude toward the goods of creation—not just the obvious products of the earth, like plants and animals, but also things we describe as human-made, like clothes, technology, and building materials—will help us seamlessly connect the importance of those goods to us with the importance, the dignity, of the workers who made them.

The idea that an item can represent the labor and bear the dignity of its creator is found throughout Catholicism's sacred texts and prayer practices. In the Bible, God refers to the chosen people as "the bud of my planting, my handiwork to show my glory" (Isa. 60:21, NAB) and they respond: "[W]e are the clay and you the potter: we are all the work of your hands" (Isa. 64:7). Both images simultaneously evoke the finished product and the work that took place to make it, wrapping product and process into one image of precious goodness. The *Book of Blessings* published by the US Catholic Bishops contains prayers for blessing many ordinary items, including transportation vehicles, boats and fishing tackle, and "technical installations or equipment."[73] The blessing for work tools comments, "This blessing has reference not so much to the objects but to the people who will use them in their work."[74] These prayers help Catholics see, in their use of ordinary items, the dignity of workers and their role in God's plan for creation.

A sacramental approach to the food we consume would start with buying only what we need and using all of it, respecting farmworkers' labor by reducing our food waste. Wasting food consumes environmental resources needlessly, contributes to global warming, takes up landfill space, and strikes us as callous while people are going hungry. As Pope Francis wrote,

> Food waste, one of the most serious forms of waste generation, also shows an arrogant disregard for everything that, in social and human terms, lies behind food production. Throwing food away means failing to value the sacrifice, labor, transport and energy costs involved in bringing quality food to the table. It means disregarding all those who work hard every day in the agricultural, industrial and service sectors to provide food that was lost or wasted and did not achieve its laudable purpose.[75]

When we see food as the sacramental representation of human labor, we can recognize that wasting it disrespects the agricultural workers whose labor made it possible for us to eat. Someone bent their back to get me those berries while they're fresh and good, at a price I can afford; the least I can do is eat and enjoy them before they spoil. With a sacramental view of the goods of creation, enjoying our meals can become a daily reminder to advocate for more just policies for food workers, expecting the government as indirect employer to pursue food security without treating these essential workers as disposable.

A sacramental view of the goods of creation reminds us that our purchases can support good working conditions when we strive to the extent possible to choose goods made in conditions that respect human dignity. Both Cavanaugh and theologian Tom Beaudoin suggest purchasing from "fair trade" and other verifiably ethical producers and developing our awareness of the conditions in which our goods are made.[76] David Cloutier suggests that while justly made goods usually cost more, this is a better use of any surplus income we might have than the "little luxuries" we easily justify.[77] The complex global supply chains in which we participate, and the awareness that our purchases likely contribute to injustice at many stages along the line, can become overwhelming. However, rather than giving in to despair, these reminders to think carefully about our consumption and use of disposable income can remind us that the opportunity to exercise worker solidarity happens daily. As theologian Laura Hartman writes, "If I exercise frugality, temperance, and generosity, this will likely benefit my neighbors whether I know who they are or not."[78] The ability to purchase products made in conditions of dignity, even just a daily cup of coffee, provides a concrete way to experience ourselves not as passive participants, but as actors for justice in the global economy.

The same respect for the item that conveys the hard work of the humans who created it applies to nonfood items. As with food, we can choose purchases carefully and use them in ways that respect the labor that produced them. The "right to repair" movement advocates for customers to have access to parts and plans needed to repair their own electronics. Pressuring manufacturers to make it easier for us to repair items instead of throwing them away respects the environment and workers' labor. Repairing an appliance or mending a garment or shoe expresses that the energy and ingenuity workers put into making an item are not valueless because some small aspect of the item becomes unsatisfactory. Businesses that repair clothing, shoes, and appliances, although they are increasingly rare, are often small and owner-operated. Spending money there supports workers in a situation where they have input into their own working conditions, aligned with the Catholic social teaching principles of dignity of work and subsidiarity. At a larger scale, a growing movement in favor of "deconstruction" advocates for demolishing buildings carefully, saving construction materials for reuse instead of sending them to landfills. This practice indicates respect for the materials of creation and the workers who built the structure years ago.

A sacramental view of the materials of creation would suggest we dispose of unwanted items in a way that respects the resources and work that produced them, either by passing them on to someone else through resale or donation or through recycling. Burying items in landfills or dumping them in the ocean, harming the environment while limiting the item's lifespan of utility, should be practices of last resort. I am active in my local Buy Nothing group, where neighbors use social media to find new homes for everything from furniture and toys to leftover pie or unwanted shampoo. I doubt most Buy Nothing members would use a word like "sacramental" to describe how they see their own and other people's stuff. But many are motivated by environmental concerns, seeking a longer life outside the landfill for the earth's resources that produced their items, and others by concern for their community, seeing the objects they pass along as a way to nurture relationships with neighbors. This care to avoid waste and connect still-useful items with those who can use them has a sacramental character.

Conclusion

Catholic social teaching's inclusive definition of work can be perplexing, as we might ask, "Is there any human activity that is not work? And what's the point of defining everything we do as work?" But understanding that work describes both the labor we are paid for on the job and what might feel like the very different tasks of cooking or completing chores at home can help us improve our thinking about the balance of activities we need for a well-lived life.

We might struggle less with the conflict between unpaid and paid work if we were able to recognize that both are work, with the demands and rewards that work can offer us. This might mean treating unpaid home work, including food work, as seriously as paid work—building it intentionally into our schedule along with paid work and rest, and dividing it equitably between household members. At the same time, we can recognize that home food work and other forms of unpaid labor can serve our well-being by helping us experience flow and complete the stress cycle. This work challenges us in a positive way when we "subdue the earth" by transforming the materials of creation. God created these goods to serve the needs of all people, which Catholic social teaching underscores by calling for large holdings of farmland, *latifundia*, to be redistributed to farmers if they are not being used. In the US context as well, the government as indirect employer has a great deal of responsibility for the too-often dangerous and unjust conditions of paid food work, which points toward advocacy as a way to make these jobs better. We can help the materials of creation meet their purpose by treating them respectfully as the products of labor they are. A sacramental view of the goods of creation would both invite us to immerse ourselves more fully in our unpaid food work, recognizing how the results contain and convey our labor for ourselves and our loved ones, and encourage us to pursue justice and flourishing for the workers whose labor feeds us.

Notes

1. Khristopher J. Brooks, "These Are the Most Dangerous Jobs in America," *CBS News*, April 30, 2024, https://www.cbsnews.com/news/dangerous-deadly-jobs-list-2024-osha/.
2. Sessions & Kimball, "U.S. Sexual Harassment Statistics," *Sessions & Kimball LLP* (blog), October 21, 2022, https://www.job-law.com/sexual-harassment-statistics/.
3. n.a., "Employer-Reported Workplace Injuries and Illnesses (Annual) News Release—2022 A01 Results," *Bureau of Labor Statistics*, November 8, 2023, https://www.bls.gov/news.release/archives/osh_11082023.htm.
4. Michael Sainato, "'A Lot of Abuse for Little Pay': How US Farming Profits from Exploitation and Brutality," *The Guardian*, December 25, 2021, https://www.theguardian.com/us-news/2021/dec/25/us-farms-made-200m-human-smuggling-labor-trafficking-operation; Melissa Sanchez Jameel Maryam, "Death on a Dairy Farm: What Really Happened to 8-Year-Old Jefferson Rodríguez," *ProPublica*, February 23, 2023, https://www.propublica.org/article/wisconsin-dairy-farm-jefferson-rodriguez.

5   n.a., "Ag and Food Sectors and the Economy," *USDA Economic Research Service*, December 19, 2024, https://www.ers.usda.gov/data-products/ag-and-food-statistics-charting-the-essentials/ag-and-food-sectors-and-the-economy/; n.a., "Almost Half the World's Population Lives in Households Linked to Agrifood Systems," *Food and Agriculture Organization of the United Nations*, March 4, 2023, https://www.fao.org/newsroom/detail/almost-half-the-world-s-population-lives-in-households-linked-to-agrifood-systems.

6   Lindsey Smith Taillie, "Who's Cooking? Trends in US Home Food Preparation by Gender, Education, and Race/Ethnicity from 2003 to 2016," *Nutrition Journal* 17, no. 1 (April 2, 2018): 41, https://doi.org/10.1186/s12937-018-0347-9.

7   Meg St-Esprit, "Why Is Making Dinner So Hard?," *Gloria*, October 18, 2023, https://www.hellogloria.com/essays/the-mental-load-of-dinner.

8   Nicholas Zill, "What Couples with Children Argue About Most," *Institute for Family Studies*, July 29, 2020, https://ifstudies.org/blog/what-couples-with-children-argue-about-most.

9   Anastacia Marx de Salcedo, *In Defense of Processed Food* (London: Reaktion Books, 2023), 56.

10 No, I do not normally bake my own sandwich bread! 2020 was an unusual time.

11 Deb Perelman, "Potatoes Anna," *Smitten Kitchen*, May 16, 2017, https://smittenkitchen.com/2017/05/potatoes-anna/.

12 Mihaly Csikszentmihalyi, *Flow: The Psychology of Optimal Experience* (New York: Harper & Row, 1990), 39–42.

13 Csikszentmihalyi, *Flow*, 53.

14 Csikszentmihalyi, *Flow*, 72.

15 Csikszentmihalyi, *Flow*, 53.

16 Csikszentmihalyi, *Flow*, 53.

17 Csikszentmihalyi, *Flow*, 159.

18 Csikszentmihalyi, *Flow*, 160.

19 Csikszentmihalyi, *Flow*.

20 Michael Y. Park, "A History of the Cake Mix, the Invention That Redefined 'Baking,'" Bon Appétit, September 26, 2013, https://www.bonappetit.com/entertaining-style/pop-culture/article/cake-mix-history Park debunks a version of this story I had heard elsewhere, that the transformative innovation was requiring bakers to crack an egg. In fact, while it's always been possible to make cake mixes with dried eggs, most manufacturers reintroduced fresh eggs into their recipes fairly early in the development of cake mix.

21 I don't mean to overlook the continued, and shameful, existence of food insecurity, just to point out that the infrastructure of connecting people with food is a major project of the business, government, and nonprofit sectors, in a way that cannot be said of assuring access to sports, games, or the arts, for example.
22 Thanks to my colleague Rachel Detert for introducing me to the work of the Nagoski sisters.
23 Emily Nagoski and Amelia Nagoski, *Burnout: The Secret to Unlocking the Stress Cycle* (New York: Ballantine Books, 2019), 5–13.
24 Nagoski and Nagoski, *Burnout*, 15.
25 Nagoski and Nagoski, *Burnout*, 18.
26 Nagoski and Nagoski, *Burnout*, 25.
27 Nagoski and Nagoski, *Burnout*, 25.
28 Rebecca May Johnson, *Small Fires: An Epic in the Kitchen* (London: Pushkin Press, 2023), 51.
29 Crawford, *Shop Class as Soulcraft*, 21–22.
30 Crawford, *Shop Class as Soulcraft*, 98.
31 Johnson, *Small Fires*, 135.
32 Anthony Annett, *Cathonomics: How Catholic Tradition Can Create a More Just Economy* (Washington, DC: Georgetown University Press, 2022), chapter 5 provides a good breakdown of this aspect of the tradition.
33 Matthew Philipp Whelan, *Blood in the Fields: Óscar Romero, Catholic Social Teaching, and Land Reform* (Washington, D.C.: Catholic University of America, 2022), 56, https://web.p.ebscohost.com/ehost/ebookviewer/ebook/bmxlYmtfXzIzNzU1ODdfX0FO0?sid=edd4e48e-f4ad-40ef-af57-53b5a9ff932c@redis&vid=0&format=EB&rid=1.
34 Whelan, *Blood in the Fields*, 56; on sharecropping, see Jennifer Jensen Wallach, *Getting What We Need Ourselves: How Food Has Shaped African American Life* (Lanham, MD: Rowman & Littlefield, 2022).
35 Wallach, *Getting What We Need Ourselves*, 58.
36 Wallach, *Getting What We Need Ourselves*, 62.
37 Wallach, *Getting What We Need Ourselves*, 59.
38 Taxation is not the same as expropriation, which is intended to deprive the original owner of an entire property, rather than a portion of the property or of its value. Tracey Epps, "Taxation and Expropriation," *Otago Law Review* 13, no. 1 (2013): 145.
39 Paul VI, "Populorum Progressio (On the Development of Peoples)," March 26, 1967, para. 24, http://www.vatican.va/content/paul-vi/en/encyclicals/documents/hf_p-vi_enc_26967_populorum.html; John

Paul II, "Laborem Exercens: On Human Work," September 14, 1981, para. 21, http://www.vatican.va/holy_father/john_paul_ii/encyclicals/documents/hf_jp-ii_enc_14091981_laborem-exercens_en.html.

40 Peter Knox, "Pope Francis and the Land Issue in Africa," *African Forum: Catholic Theological Ethics in the World Church* (blog), accessed May 7, 2024, https://catholicethics.com/forum/pope-francis-and-the-land-issue-in-africa/.

41 Pontifical Council for Justice and Peace, "Towards a Better Distribution of Land: The Challenge of Agrarian Reform" (Libreria Editrice Vaticana, November 23, 1997), 33, http://www.vatican.va/roman_curia/pontifical_councils/justpeace/documents/rc_pc_justpeace_doc_12011998_distribuzione-terra_en.html.

42 Pontifical Council for Justice and Peace, 19–21.

43 Pontifical Council for Justice and Peace, 37–38.

44 Pontifical Council for Justice and Peace, 36. The document is careful to note that expropriation of large landholdings is not a sufficient solution to injustices in the agricultural sphere; legal protections for small family farmers, improved infrastructure investment and trade policies, and many other solutions are also needed to honor the labor of agricultural workers and safeguard their rights.

45 U.S. Conference of Catholic Bishops, "Economic Justice for All: Pastoral Letter on Catholic Social Teaching and the U.S. Economy," 1986, 217, http://www.usccb.org/upload/economic_justice_for_all.pdf.

46 Sainato, "A Lot of Abuse for Little Pay."

47 Maryam Jameel Sanchez Melissa, "No Right to Medical Care, Compensation for Injuries or Time Off: How Immigrant Dairy Workers Go From Vital to Disposable," *ProPublica*, December 20, 2023, https://www.propublica.org/article/wisconsin-dairy-farm-immigrant-workers-injury-safety.

48 Brooks, "These Are the Most Dangerous Jobs in America."

49 Michael Sainato, "While Other Sectors Experience Strikes, Farm Workers Are Still Fighting for Basic Human Rights," *The Real News Network*, November 4, 2021, http://therealnews.com/while-other-sectors-experience-strikes-farm-workers-are-still-fighting-for-basic-human-rights.

50 Nichole M. Flores, "The Invisible Woman: Seeing Migrant Women through the Eyes of Christ," *America Magazine* 209, no. 12 (October 28, 2013): 41–42.

51 Timothy Pachirat, *Every Twelve Seconds: Industrialized Slaughter and the Politics of Sight* (New Haven, CT: Yale University Press, 2013), 11, 104.

52 Sangaramoorthy, Thurka. "Liminal Living: Everyday Injury, Disability, and Instability among Migrant Mexican Women in Maryland's Seafood Industry." *Medical Anthropology Quarterly* 33, no. 4 (2019): 557–78. https://doi.org/10.1111/maq.12526.
53 "2023—Minimum Wages for Tipped Employees," *U.S. Department of Labor*, accessed June 4, 2024, https://www.dol.gov/agencies/whd/state/minimum-wage/tipped/2023.
54 Emily Guendelsberger, *On the Clock: What Low-Wage Work Did to Me and How It Drives America Insane* (New York: Little, Brown and Company, 2019), 277.
55 Pachirat, *Every Twelve Seconds*.
56 Tracie McMillan, *The American Way of Eating: Undercover at Walmart, Applebee's, Farm Fields and the Dinner Table* (New York: Scribner, 2012), chaps. 1–4.
57 Sainato, "While Other Sectors Experience Strikes, Farm Workers Are Still Fighting for Basic Human Rights."
58 Sainato, "A Lot of Abuse for Little Pay."
59 Alyssa Battistoni, "America Spends Less on Food Than Any Other Country," *Mother Jones* (blog) https://www.motherjones.com/food/2012/02/america-food-spending-less/ (accessed May 16, 2024).
60 Linda Qiu, "Meatpackers Misled Public and Influenced Trump Administration During Covid, Report Says," *The New York Times*, May 12, 2022, https://www.nytimes.com/2022/05/12/us/politics/meatpackers-trump-covid.html.
61 Albino Barrera, "Gaudium et Spes and Catholic Ethics in Post-Industrial Economics: Indirect Employers and Globalization," *Journal of Catholic Social Thought* 3, no. 2 (October 1, 2006): 323, https://doi.org/10.5840/jcathsoc20063226; Without using the term "indirect employer," Daniel K. Finn, *Consumer Ethics in a Global Economy: How Buying Here Causes Injustice There* (Washington, DC: Georgetown University Press, 2019) thoughtfully unpacks the way individual consumers can be seen as contributing to working conditions within the global economy.
62 E.g., Dominic Farrell, "Does the Principle of Cooperation in Wrongdoing Work When Assessing Economic Complicity?," *Journal of Markets & Morality* 22, no. 1 (2019): 99–116.
63 n.a., "Key Campaigns," *UFW* (blog), n.d., https://ufw.org/organizing/key-campaigns/.
64 "About CIW," *Coalition of Immokalee Workers*, March 14, 2013, https://ciw-online.org/about/.
65 Marx de Salcedo, *In Defense of Processed Food*, 64–5.

66 Helen Hester and Nick Srnicek, *After Work: A History of the Home and the Fight for Free Time* (New York: Verso, 2023), 174–6. I am not convinced this solution is preferable to changes that would ensure all workers have enough disposable income to patronize their local restaurant or supermarket "hot bar," provided that the workers producing food in those workplaces are themselves treated justly.

67 William T. Cavanaugh, *Being Consumed: Economics and Christian Desire* (Grand Rapids, MI: William B. Eerdmans Publishing Company, 2008), 57.

68 Dorothy Day, "On Pilgrimage: December [1948]," *The Catholic Worker*, December 5, 1948, https://catholicworker.org/486-html/.

69 Deb Perelman, "Chicken Rice with Buttered Onions," *Smitten Kitchen*, September 28, 2023, https://smittenkitchen.com/2023/09/chicken-rice-with-buttered-onions/.

70 Mike Powell, "Letter of Recommendation: Washing Dishes," *The New York Times*, June 4, 2019, https://www.nytimes.com/2019/06/04/magazine/letter-of-recommendation-washing-dishes.html.

71 Addison Del Mastro, "Kitchen Break," Substack newsletter, *The Deleted Scenes* (blog), May 27, 2024, https://thedeletedscenes.substack.com/p/kitchen-break?publication_id=329870&utm_campaign=email-post-title&r=7f1&utm_medium=email.

72 Susan A. Ross, *Extravagant Affections: A Feminist Sacramental Theology*, Reprint ed. (New York: Continuum, 2001), 141.

73 International Commission on English in the Liturgy, *Book of Blessings: Abridged Edition* (Collegeville, MN: Liturgical Press, 1990), 283–324, at 305.

74 International Commission on English in the Liturgy, 319.

75 Pope Francis, "Message of the Holy Father Francis to the Director General of the FAO for the International Day of Awareness of Food Loss and Waste 2023," *Vatican.va*, September 29, 2023, https://press.vatican.va/content/salastampa/en/bollettino/pubblico/2023/09/29/230929g.html.

76 Cavanaugh, *Being Consumed*, 57–58; Tom Beaudoin, *Consuming Faith: Integrating Who We Are with What We Buy*, 2nd ed. (Lanham, MD: Sheed & Ward, 2006), 99–100.

77 David Cloutier, *The Vice of Luxury: Economic Excess in a Consumer Age* (Washington, D.C.: Georgetown University Press, 2015), 36–37.

78 Laura M. Hartman, *The Christian Consumer: Living Faithfully in a Fragile World* (New York: Oxford University Press, 2011), 123.

5
Do Artists Work? Creativity and Leisure

Chapter Outline

Leisure: The Importance of Doing Nothing	96
Artists' Insights on Work and Doing Nothing	102
Structures for Leisure	110
Conclusion	115

Creating art is a good example of why the common definition of work as what we do for pay is so inadequate. Artmaking is a creative human activity that demands significant time, focus, and skill development, but many people see it as not work, but something else—a side gig at best, or simply a hobby. Artists describe their experience in terms that overlap with the ways Catholic thought sees both work, which is active and shapes the world, and leisure, where we slow down and pay attention to the world and ourselves.[1] Catholic thought on leisure has a lot in common with the insights of recent best-selling books on resisting the cultural pressure toward constant activity. Together, these perspectives help us see how we can fully appreciate how work is good for us while knowing that it's good to *not* work sometimes, too. This chapter incorporates interviews with working artists to explore work's restorative quality, the intrinsic motivation to work, and the necessity of non-working time to restore ourselves and our creativity. There are actions we can take on our own to protect our non-working time; we need to examine our attitudes toward work and productivity and do what we can to balance work with restorative non-work time. However, the deep human need for leisure to restore ourselves also calls for communities to build structures of support for nonworking time, from changed cultural attitudes to financial support for those not currently working.

Leisure: The Importance of Doing Nothing

If you asked people today why so many of us feel pressure to be constantly busy and productive, and even believe that our worth as a person rests on our productivity, they might offer one of two reasons. Some people truly do need to work constantly in order to afford to survive, while others don't but have accepted the internal attitude that our worth is tied to our productivity. The philosopher Josef Pieper would add a third reason: it could be that a totalitarian state requires them to be constantly working.[2] This was a situation he knew from experience.

Josef Pieper (1904–1997), a Catholic philosopher, was an early-career academic in Germany when Hitler came to power. Many professors who were part of the Catholic minority in Germany supported the Third Reich and worked hard to show connections between Catholic thought and Nazi ideology.[3] Pieper did not do this. At the same time, while he voted against the Nazi Party, he was not a brave member of the resistance. He seems to have spent Hitler's rule trying to survive as best he could, figuring out how to support his family as a writer under a regime that banned any publications less than fully supportive of fascism.[4] For a time, he worked for the Third Reich army evaluating the health of draftees, a job he took to avoid being drafted to fight himself.[5] It seems to me that his choices during these years certainly do not mark him out as a brave resistor of totalitarianism, but also do not expose him as a willing collaborator with the Nazis.

The Nazis equated human worth with productivity, murdering persons deemed "defective" and trying to direct every worker's energy to serving the fascist state. Pieper's best-known work today, which argued that we need leisure to remain truly human, can certainly be seen as opposed to their ideology, as well as to the capitalist consumerism that became widespread after the Second World War. Pieper's advocacy of leisure opposed what he called "the world of total work," in which we associate human worth with economic productivity and frantic activity (and which could exist in capitalist or totalitarian economies). Leisure was not simply rest, but a conscious state; not simply play, but deep reflection on the world; not simply a break to refresh ourselves to return to work, but something whose importance is innate, not related to work at all. Pieper is not talking about "leisure time," as in free time when we are not working. While time off is certainly important, leisure, what he's talking about, is a state of mind.

In work, Pieper says, we are active; we expend effort; and we achieve something for the good of society. In leisure, by contrast, we are non-active, accepting the world as it is and celebrating what is good in it, rather than working to change it. In work, we make a contribution; in leisure, we receive, resting in the goodness of our self, our relationships, the resources we have to enjoy, and the life that God gives us. Work itself is not bad for us; no Catholic philosopher could make that claim. What Pieper did see as deeply harmful is "the world of total work," the cultural insistence that things—and people—can only be valued if they are economically productive.

Leisure reflects the very real fact that as God's creatures, we have received ourselves as a gift. In work, we put that gift to service for the sake of others, but in leisure, we remind ourselves that we are a gift, and we celebrate that. An example of leisure is contemplation, the deep, curious enjoyment of something beautiful, intriguing, awe-inspiring, or not fully known. Leisure is an intentionally non-productive state of mind that can, paradoxically, help us generate new ideas: "Leisure implies an attitude of total receptivity toward, and willing immersion in, reality; an openness of the soul, through which alone may come about those great and blessed insights that no amount of 'mental labor' can ever achieve."[6] Pieper may distinguish leisure from work as non-active, but it is not passive; when we leisure, we are engaged, with our self caught up in what we are doing. Sleep is important rest, but it isn't leisure.

Pieper distinguishes leisure from a "break from work." A break takes its structure, meaning, and purpose from work, refreshing our bodies and minds so we can return to our work in the future. Breaks are important, but not the same as leisure, which exists for its own intrinsic value, not for the sake of work.[7] "When we really let our minds rest contemplatively on a rose in bud, on a child at play, on a divine mystery, we are rested and quickened as though by a dreamless sleep."[8] Theologian Christine Firer Hinze gives us useful terms for contrasting leisure and breaks from work: rest-amid and rest-apart.[9] "Rest amid" our daily activities points to the refreshment that can come even while we are doing work. Examples are flow achieved during work or a break with the purpose of returning to work.[10] By contrast, "rest-apart occurs in times and places when one ceases striving and puts aside work-related activities."[11] Similar to leisure, rest-apart is not directed toward restoring ourselves for work. Even though we may find renewal in moments while doing our daily work, the times we intentionally block out for rest have a different significance, reminding us that our worth does not come from our productivity.

Leisure is more of a state of mind than an activity, but certain activities can invite us to leisure more than others. Examples include celebrating a festival or feast, which take us out of the everyday to celebrate the world and ourselves within it. The highest action in pursuit of leisure is worshipping God, which creates a space and a practice "absolutely antithetic to utility," the ultimate rejection of the world of total work.[12] While refreshing us, leisure is a way to celebrate who we are, being "at one" with ourselves and restfully accepting our own being.[13]

Pieper contrasts this self-accepting state with *acedia*, which translates to "lack of care," and is understood in the Christian tradition as a state of sin.[14] Distinct from the joyful, attentive nonactivity that characterizes leisure, *acedia* is an unpleasant state where we are neither relaxing nor engaged in satisfying work, but unhappily occupied chasing after distraction or stimulus. (The compulsive, anxious feeling of scrolling social media long after we should have started work or gone to bed is a modern example.) If leisure is accepting who we are, the inability to settle down to work or rest that is *acedia* indicates a failure to accept our own nature.

Interestingly, psychologist Csikszentmihalyi evaluated the modern use of free time in terms that echo Pieper's criticism of *acedia*. Unlike paid work, where the challenge can lead us into the pleasant state of flow,

> Free time . . . is unstructured, and requires much greater effort to shape itself into something that can be enjoyed. Hobbies that demand skill, habits that set goals and limits, personal interests, and especially inner discipline

> help to make [free time] what it is supposed to be—a chance for *re-creation*. . . . Nevertheless, instead of using our physical and mental resources to experience flow, most of us spend many hours each week watching celebrated athletes play in enormous stadiums. Instead of making music, we listen to platinum records cut by millionaire musicians. . . . We do not run risks acting on our beliefs, but occupy hours each day watching actors who pretend to have adventures, engaged in mock-meaningful action.[15]

Csikszentmihalyi's unsparing account of the modern use of free time suggests that many of us prefer distraction from our own bodies, lives, and companions over fully and presently engaging with those gifts. If we played sports or instruments, or joined social movements, instead of spending our free time passively, we could expect our free time to grant us more of the rest-amid that comes through the experience of flow. And of course, playing sports or music or taking civic action all qualify as work in Catholic social teaching's inclusive definition. Catholic social teaching agrees with Csikszentmihalyi's suggestion: work is good for us. We experience this unmistakably when we find ourselves restored by engaging in work activities during our free time.

Theologian Conor Kelly suggests that we could understand leisure as a flow experience that arises during non-work time, although "all leisure experiences will be experiences of flow, but not all flow experiences will be experiences of leisure."[16] For example, "flow" experiences at a paid job do not stem from a freely chosen decision to "let go," as Pieper would describe it, so while they may be restful, they are not leisure. Kelly urges us to be thoughtful about how we spend our free time—when we're not engaged in either paid or unpaid work—to carve out time when the receptive, celebratory experience of leisure is likely to find us. To best set ourselves up to experience leisure, he advises seeking flow during time with God, time with self, and time with others.[17]

I believe Kelly is right that leisure, as Pieper describes it, can feel like flow, but I worry that making flow the key test of leisure runs the risk of collapsing leisure into work. Csikszentmihalyi himself noted that it's easier to achieve flow at work, where we challenge our skills by pursuing external standards, than in our free time when we must set our own goals and choose our own activities.[18] For me, the key feature of leisure is that we achieve it during activities that are deliberately nonproductive—in fact, that couldn't possibly be seen as productive. If you are exercising to change your body's strength or shape, you might well achieve flow during the activity (which would then be rest-amid). But that activity is still work, not leisure; you can't celebrate something for what it is at the same time you are working to change it. In contrast, we could pursue leisure by taking a walk in the woods with the intention of gratefully celebrating our body and soul. To an outside observer, this might even look like exercise. But exercise has an end that is not intrinsic to its own action: the goal of changing our body's performance or shape. Leisure is an end in itself.

This matters, not because we must follow Pieper's definition of leisure at all costs, but because our society already places too high a value on work, on our ability to be productive and generate change. Pieper's insistence that we need times of acceptance, receptivity, and active celebration of what is—what is right now, without trying to change it—is a desperately needed corrective to our obsession with productivity.

Pieper's insights on leisure—how good it is for us; how we can pursue it; and how hard it is to do so given the extremely high value modern culture places on work and activity—are strikingly similar to the thought of two contemporary artists and thought leaders, Tricia Hersey and Jenny Odell. Hersey is an artist and theologian with a master's degree in divinity, who founded The Nap Ministry to uphold the spiritual, personal, and political importance of intentional rest, especially for Black and Brown people. Odell is an artist and writer whose work argues that self-consciously nonproductive activity, like taking the time to notice the nature and creatures around you, can restore our creativity and communities. Each artist has laid forth her philosophy in a bestselling book.

Hersey's framework of thought lends its title to her book: *Rest Is Resistance*. To rest is to resist capitalism, white supremacy, and "grind culture," which treat human bodies as tools for profit, ignoring human well-being.[19] Hersey points out that "sleep deprivation is a public health issue," especially for marginalized communities.[20] Making the practice of rest as resistance visible, The Nap Ministry hosts public events where people are invited to literally nap, with pillows, blankets, and soothing music. But Hersey defines rest more broadly than sleep: it can include focusing on nature outside or through a window, daydreaming, enjoying music and art, and prayer.[21] An intentional break from social media is both rest from the frantic activity of scrolling and resistance to the tech companies whose algorithms commodify our attention.[22]

As with Pieper's leisure, rest for Hersey does not have work as a goal. "The Rest Is Resistance framework . . . does not believe in the toxic idea that we are resting to recharge and rejuvenate so we can be prepared to give more output to capitalism. . . . We are not resting to be productive."[23] Again paralleling Pieper's leisure, Hersey insists that "rest makes us more human. It brings us back to our human-ness."[24] All the qualities that make life truly human must be preceded by rest: "How can we access pleasure, joy and liberation if we are too tired to experience it?"[25] Finally, rest supports imagination—not simply daydreaming, but a powerful tool for social change. Through rest, we tap into our imagination and become able to see that another world is possible.[26]

In her own manifesto *How To Do Nothing*, Jenny Odell discusses the power of paying sustained attention to something outside yourself, and the insights, awareness, and gratitude that arise during what looks like "doing nothing." Odell, an artist whose practice encompasses installation, digital art, and writing, advocates "doing nothing" as resistance to capitalism, particularly to the "attention economy" which extracts our attention through persuasive algorithms and sells it back to us at a profit. An example of "doing nothing" is bird-watching, or what Odell calls "bird-noticing," an unproductive act that becomes progressively more rewarding as we give it patient, sustained attention over time.[27] Another is the slow tuning in that takes place while enjoying a work of art or a walk in the woods. As with Pieper's leisure and Hersey's rest, "the point of 'doing nothing,'" Odell says, "isn't to return to work refreshed and ready to be more productive, but rather to question what we currently perceive as productive. . . . From either a social or ecological perspective, the ultimate goal of 'doing nothing' is to wrest our focus from the attention economy and replant it in the public, physical realm."[28]

Compared to Pieper and Hersey, Odell says less about how "doing nothing" supports an individual person's well-being. She seems to see it more as a practice for the common good, a way to practice responsible use of our attention so we can use it wisely to work toward a better world. We must be able to focus our attention on one thing if we are to unite our efforts with others in movements for social change.[29] "'Doing nothing'—in the sense of refusing productivity and stopping to listen—entails an active process of listening that seeks out the effects of racial, environmental, and economic injustice and brings about real change."[30]

For Odell, "doing nothing" is a necessary precondition to resistance. For Pieper and Hersey, the practices of leisure or rest are, in themselves, resistance to life-destroying expectations within society. Hersey positions rest as a weapon against capitalism and what she calls "grind culture," the idea that we can thrive within capitalism through constant work. For Pieper, the "world of total work" is both external and internal, imposed by cultural norms and economic conditions, and also self-imposed when we accept that our worth is tied to our productivity. He warned against a voluntary "inner impoverishment," when we accept the world of total work, not because we are forced to by poverty or politics, but because we simply lack the imagination to envision anything more to life than work.[31] Both Pieper and Hersey blame our inability to rest on both economic realities outside ourselves and our own voluntary acceptance of those conditions.

Unlike Hersey and Odell, Pieper does not explicitly talk about how leisure is important for social justice. However, he does see leisure as a potential source of great insight and as something that keeps us human. Hersey, Odell, and Pieper all agree: taking time away from work to intentionally be unproductive is necessary for our own well-being and helps shape us into the type of person we are meant to be, someone capable of valuing life's gifts beyond work and living in accordance with those values.

Artists' Insights on Work and Doing Nothing

I try to teach Pieper's thinking on leisure in all of my classes to remind my students, who are often stressed about achieving good grades and careers, that they are worthy above and beyond their own productivity. It always takes us a while to grapple with his idea that leisure exists only for its own sake, not for productivity or for restoring us for work. Although leisure is a state of mind, it matters that we choose to pursue it through deliberately unproductive activities. We look at some examples: a walk in the woods could be an opportunity to "celebrate the world as it is," but not if you're doing it for fitness or taking observations for your biology thesis.

Meditation could produce leisure, but if you're meditating to keep from going back to the office and punching your belittling boss, you're doing it for the sake of work. Another example that I've always struggled with myself: could making art be a way to pursue leisure?

Artmaking has a good case for being considered work in Catholic social teaching. Work is a way we imitate God the Creator, and art is the ultimate creative activity. It transforms the materials of creation and transforms the artist as they practice and develop their skills. On the other hand, since many artists have income-earning "day jobs" to support their creative practice, art falls short of the widely accepted definition of work as what you do for pay. Could artmaking be a way to access leisure? After all, it is a way of paying attention to and honoring the world as it is, and often an activity where the artist "lets herself go under," experiencing flow. *Enjoying* art certainly seems to be a leisure activity.[32] Hersey, Odell, and Pieper's books are filled with references to their favorite paintings, music, and performances, and the way these works invite them to pay attention, celebrating the world and their own place in it. Not an artist myself, I could not resolve whether the experience of artmaking was closer to work or to leisure, and I really wanted a more definitive answer to give my students. So, I asked some artists.

This section of the chapter is based on interviews with artists from the Milwaukee and Chicago areas. Obviously, their views can't represent everyone with an artistic practice, though I was struck by the diversity of thoughts and experiences just among the few folks who were kind enough to share their insights with me. As you'll see, many, though not all, believe that artmaking is a form of work. They beautifully articulate how their creative work can afford opportunities for rest-amid, something all workers can aspire to. And they all agree on the importance of something like leisure: intentional, nonproductive time that is good for the person and their creative expression. Their insights clearly point away from Pieper's "world of total work": art is something that has to be done for its own sake, not to fulfill a need for food, money, or anything else. The deep intrinsic motivation that these artists have for their work is something Catholic thought believes every person is capable of. After speaking with them, I now am convinced that artmaking is work, not leisure.

The majority of the artists I spoke with quickly agreed that they see their art as work. Anja Notanja Sieger is a Milwaukee artist whose multigenre practice spans printmaking, shadow puppetry, typewriter poetry, and more. Sieger sees work in general as combining elements of "vocation ... what gives people meaning in life" and "elbow grease," the more tedious or repetitive aspects.[33] For her, art-making is vocational work, but it also involves an elbow grease requirement. Adebisi Agoro, a Milwaukee hip-hop artist who performs as BLAX, concurs, pointing to the consistency and strategic thinking needed to develop a body of work and an audience.[34] The repetition needed to move toward excellence also marks art-making as work for Nick Garcia, a Chicago writer whose work encompasses poetry, prose, comedy, and hip-hop. At first, Garcia was not sure about identifying art with work, remarking that at work "I need to do things that I'd rather not do, that are not stimulating to me, that are sometimes tedious, that are sometimes stressful." On the other hand, artistic practice can demand a similar discipline: "Creative people can create all day, but you have to also learn to stop. You have to learn to go back and edit your stuff—you kind of have to do stuff that does feel like work."[35]

Matthew Bailey, a Milwaukee-based visual artist, pointed out that the same activity can be viewed as a job or a hobby depending on how much time the person spends on it. For example, someone who spends forty hours or more a week tending plants is considered a farmer, but if it's only a few hours a week, we see that as the hobby of gardening. Art is often taken less seriously than other occupations in terms of compensation; someone might offer to pay a plumber friend who does work for them but expect an artist to do the same favor for "fun." "To ask somebody who spends more than 40 hours a week doing something whether or not that's work, that seems problematic," Bailey offers. "I do everything that a person would do in a job with the exception of getting paid the way I want ... you keep certain hours, you're devoted to it, it occupies your time and thoughts ... I definitely think anybody that you see that puts this much of themselves into an activity, it should be regarded as work."[36]

Matthew Filipowicz, a comedian and satirist in Milwaukee (and, full disclosure, my husband), differentiated between the work needed to organize and promote comedy shows and the performance itself: "Once I'm on stage, it does not feel like work. It's just fun. And play."[37] But for Agoro, performing "*is* the work. . . . The performance is the ultimate manifestation of the work that has been put in. Not like any of it is grueling, hard or laborious . . . but in order for it to be a good product, there has to be work." Sieger agrees: "You always have to be strategizing . . . if you're performing, you want to always be thinking of, how is this going to be received and what will they think?" The physical after-effects of an adrenaline-inducing performance and the challenges of managing relationships with collaborators are other aspects that make performing work for Sieger.

In distinguishing artistic practice from work, Snežana Žabić, a writer and musician in Chicago, looked to the role of desire: "I think of work as something that I don't want to do." Creating or performing music or poetry does not feel like work to Žabić: "I think of it more as play. . . . It definitely doesn't feel like a job. And not just because we don't get paid, but just because it's so outside even the structure of a job." Žabić, who teaches composition to college students for her income, joked, "It's not like when I'm retired I'm going to gather a bunch of unwilling teenagers and teach them how to write academic papers!" For her, the contrast between internal and external motivation distinguished artistic practice from the "work" that one might do because of the need to earn a living.[38]

The artists I spoke with unanimously attested to a motivation to create that is a very deep part of their identity. Growing up as a refugee in Belgrade, Žabić found she was able to write even in a small apartment packed with family and their noise. The focus and joy of writing are with her still: "If I have an idea, nothing can stop me and if I don't have an idea, that's okay." Sieger reaches for the term vocation, meaning calling: "Vocation is very much the sort of thing that nobody else has to tell you what to do . . . Vocation is what you're naturally like, 'I *have* to [do].'" That sense of compulsion is echoed by other artists: Garcia says, "I can't get my brain to think about the world in a different way. I can't help it." And for Agoro, music is "just my comfortable medium of expression. I love it. I can't not do it." Filipowicz agrees: "There's part of me that needs to do something in this realm [comedy] in order for myself to feel whole . . . I don't really believe in 'meant to do,' but—I sort of do in some ways."

The powerful hold of intrinsic motivation on these artists does not keep them from thoughtfully weighing trade-offs about their time, energy, and other resources. Before conducting these interviews, I had a somewhat romanticized view of the artist as someone who creates out of an intrinsic drive, regardless of monetary compensation or other rewards. I expected to tell a story that upended the familiar association of work and pay. My interviewees thoughtfully showed me how their understanding of compensation for their artistic work is more complex than that.

Žabić finds that many writers she knows continue to create *because* they have extrinsic rewards, such as academics who must publish to advance in their careers. Without such extrinsic motivation, she believes the intrinsic drive to create can "fade away" for many: "I consider myself a minority in that I continue to do this without extrinsic rewards." Sieger also sees a complicated relationship between compensation and creativity: "As soon as you decide to go full time, you have to make work that you can sell. It's a lot more interesting to me to make art that tells a story or is funny or is weird to me and not work that fits commissions or other people's idea of what art should be." In contrast, Agoro is working toward making performance his full-time career, although he nuances that goal: "Success? It's not like a huge monetary windfall. Already, to be where I am, I'm successful. The success is just putting in the good work, you know, and if people enjoy it, it's successful." Similarly, Bailey wished for more success connecting his art with buyers, but also referenced an ironic meme about why artists create: "For respect? For money? Or so your family will be proud? None of those things apply. . . . We keep doing it [because] inspiration needs to find you working. It's like having your sail out and waiting for the wind."[39]

Fiber artist Heidi Parkes does support herself through art full-time, teaching in person and online and selling her quilts. When we met, she was earning an income as the artist in residence at the Pfister, the oldest, fanciest hotel in Milwaukee. Her conversation was peppered with references to her favorite experts in business and time management, as she has intentionally pursued the goal of being a working artist by becoming what she describes as "a little bit famous." For Parkes, the need to maintain a public persona is like a "price paid for being a working artist. . . . I felt like, if I want quilting to be my job, the way to do that is to be a person that people know." Parkes spends less time sewing than she expected when she decided to pursue art full-time, and much more time managing her web presence and online teaching. Despite the trade-offs she acknowledges in making her art her full-time job, "it feels like very exciting, satisfying work."[40]

Many artists describe their work as bringing intangible rewards that are beneficial to the person and could even be described as therapeutic. Sieger sees work as a whole, not limited to art-making, as beneficial, in terms that strikingly echo *Laborem Exercens*: "Work is good for a person." She describes the "satisfying" experience of working for pay in a warehouse, explaining that work in general is "good physically, it's good mentally and it's good just to apply yourself to the rhythm of doing something." Artmaking is particularly rewarding because it combines physical, interpersonal, and decision-making aspects, which Sieger believes are all part of the work that makes people happiest. She speaks of pursuing one's vocation as a practice of self-care: "If it's your vocation, the best gift you can give to yourself is to make room for it and to do it because you want to do it."

Other artists described the benefits of art as similar to therapy, offering the opportunity to process difficult experiences or simply to reflect on life. Parkes describes her practice of making diary quilts as "a tool for myself to live my best life and think about the things that I want to invite into my future—new ways of thinking, new neural pathways that I want to form. It's also a helpful way to reconsider the past . . . That kind of noticing helps me decide where to put . . . the limited energy of my one precious life." Similarly, for Sieger, "art has to do with finding out what it is I need to know about life right now." Žabić explains that some writers see their practice as "therapeutic" and joins in that perspective: "Figuring life out in spite of different collapses— . . . It does become a kind of a reward. You put something out in a song, or a piece of paper, and you get some kind of relief, you get some kind of therapy out of it." Bailey also volunteered "therapeutic" as a description of the rewards of artmaking, speaking of how it gives him a "sense of purpose" for confronting difficult realities like the climate crisis: "This is what I'm good at, and I can do something in the world to help bring attention to it." And Agoro movingly describes how his music helped him reconnect with his purpose, emerging from the grief and "fog" after his son died as a teenager. "I'm looking at myself and I'm like, how are you ever gonna get back to you? . . . I faced my biggest fear in my life already. So what's on the other side of fear?"

The hard, creative, personal work that is artmaking can provide an opportunity for rest-amid that restores the person and can even be therapeutic. "Therapeutic" here can mean something that heals after a sad "collapse" or a tragic loss, something that restores well-being. (This resonates with an insight shared by a colleague recovering from Long Covid, who said that her community has taught her that "rest is part of the work of healing."[41]) It can also mean something that elevates well-being above the baseline, helping us tend to important questions of self-care and purpose or envisioning new futures.

While the work of art can provide rest-amid and even therapeutic benefits, the artists I spoke with universally praised the importance of intentionally nonproductive time, with many stressing that not just artists, but all humans benefit from downtime. Garcia observes: "One huge lesson that I've learned about creativity is that it involves a lot of procrastination. . . . Sometimes that means you take a walk. Sometimes that means you've gotta go biking somewhere or go to a movie or go see a show or just have an experience." He compares the brain to a "little kid" who initially refuses to obey an adult's request, "but then you kind of walk away and then they just do it, because the problem was that you *wanted* them to do it." To "coax" your brain into creative mode, "sometimes you have to distract it." Agoro similarly suggested that the brain's creativity is not always under our conscious control, explaining that during rest, "the brain's working for you. Sometimes you just gotta stop and it's thinking for you and you wake up and I'm like, there it is!"

"Down time is a premium for making art," Sieger agrees. "You have to be able to have that stare out the window, go for walks time, and not be exhausted." Resonating with Josef Pieper, Sieger elaborates:

> Downtime is enjoying the fact that you are alive. Absorbing all that has happened to you and what you are learning in life, and connecting with yourself and how you feel. And that is important for all people, but it's also important for artists because usually when you feel no pressure and nobody needs anything from you—and maybe this is true for non-artists too—but that's when you get the spark for the next thing that pulls you along. And you can also have down time without that spark happening to you, but the spark is a lot harder to get if you don't give yourself the gift of enjoying the fact that you are alive. And you won't learn as much if you don't remember you are alive.

Intentionally nonproductive time is important not just for artists, but for everyone, Žabić observes: "It's necessary to not do anything and just kind of daydream. . . . I think that's just a basic human need." She points out that while not everyone considers themselves an artist, everyone is creative in some way: creativity basically amounts to solving problems. "Any job you're doing, or when you're taking care of others or trying to survive, it doesn't matter how you're spending your hours, you're problem solving. . . . It seems that those two are related—the intense focus on solving a problem versus periods of rest, not just sleep, but [when you're] awake, but your mind is wandering, you're daydreaming." Bailey agrees, pointing to the way babies learn by trying things 100 times and making mistakes. Similarly, for adults, "If you're searching for something that soars or something that's magic or something that goes above and beyond, you have to be handed time to play the fool."

These artists eloquently state the case for rest-apart, as well as rest-amid. Intentionally taking time away from creative pursuits and the necessity to earn an income is not only restful, it is, in an almost mysterious way, generative. "Problem solving," "coaxing" your brain to work or getting it to "think for you," receiving the "spark that pulls you along"—this complex, creative human energy does not always appear—or often does not appear—on the basis of our effort. (Parkes counsels her fiber arts students that often, "more work does not equal a more beautiful quilt.") It seems that we receive insight, in some mysterious way, when we let ourselves "go under," in Pieper's terms, and accept some time being receptive, not active. On the testimony of these artists, enjoying the fact that we are alive, remembering we are alive, in Sieger's beautiful phrasing, is not a luxury for the privileged or some quirky artistic habit, but a basic human need.

Every person is creative, though not every person will accept the challenge these artists have taken on of balancing art-making with other full-time pursuits or working to make creation their full-time job. But every worker can benefit from the insights of artists, who understand that creativity is at the heart of human nature and requires a thoughtful balance of hard work and intentional downtime for us to tap into it. When explaining the benefits they derive from their artistic practice, many of them said those goods—experiences of flow, play, or purpose—should be part of work for every person.

One of the things that concern me about the rise of generative AI is the way it erases the human person who creates and who needs a balance of work and downtime in order to do so. If we get used to the idea that we can quickly "create" a poem, image, or song with a few taps of a keyboard, we may lose sight of the insight that to be creative—to be human—requires downtime. In a similar way that manual workers, like motorcycle mechanics and cooks, remind us that we are formed and challenged in good ways when we interact with something real, artists—dedicated practitioners of the creative process—remind us that creative work can restore and heal us, and that creativity requires we take unproductive time to enjoy the fact that we are alive.

Structures for Leisure

Some would argue that pursuing leisure is a luxury for the privileged. But Tricia Hersey's embrace of the right to rest is inspired by her grandmother, who raised eight children while "dodging poverty and racism" in midcentury Chicago, and still managed to spend thirty minutes each day resting with her eyes closed, "listening for what God wants to tell me."[42] As Hersey suggests, those of us with more resources and control over our time than her grandmother Ora have fewer obstacles to seeking out time in leisure. Pieper, Hersey, and Odell mostly focus on the ways intentional nonactivity is under our own control: we must celebrate ourselves as we are; insist on our right to rest; and spend time noticing and doing nothing. However, once we've realized the importance of leisure for ourselves, it follows that every worker deserves the time and resources to engage in intentional nonactivity. We can and should build better structures for leisure.

Theologian Andrew Blosser's *The Ethics of Doing Nothing* lifts up new and old structures for supporting what he calls inoperativity, "intentional actions or states of being that have no purposive quality outside themselves," like leisure, rest, and doing nothing.[43] Blosser argues that embracing the practice of inoperativity in human life can be a key to fighting worker exploitation and even climate change, which he sees as driven by a compulsive consumerism connected to our sense that we are only worthy when we are working or spending.[44] One traditional structure to support inoperativity is the Jewish and Christian practice of Sabbath, an intentional time away from work that is not intended to restore energy for work, but exists for its own sake. To build structures that support inoperativity into our economic life, Blosser calls for universal basic income, which puts money behind the belief that people are worthy of survival even if they are not currently working.[45]

Unsurprisingly, Catholic social teaching supports the practice of Sabbath, and not just because it is a day to go to church: time off work to connect to our highest human purpose is a fundamental human right (*RN*

40-1, *QA* 135, *MM* 249-51). Christian teachings restricting work on Sunday go as far back as the Roman Empire and were primarily intended to restrict, not workers, but their employers by limiting when work could legally be required.[46] The tradition has especially insisted on the right to Sabbath for workers in particularly difficult conditions or exploitative situations, John Paul II observed, "not because this work was any less worthy when compared to the spiritual requirements of Sunday observance, but rather because it needed greater regulation to lighten its burden" (*Dies Domini* 66). He elaborated that the "right to rest" included a weekly day off as well as a longer yearly or more frequent vacation (*LE* 19). "In our own historical context there remains the obligation to ensure that everyone can enjoy the freedom, rest and relaxation which human dignity requires, together with the associated religious, family, cultural and interpersonal needs which are difficult to meet if there is no guarantee of at least one day of the week on which people can *both* rest and celebrate" (*DD* 66).

The practice of Sabbath is inspired by the Biblical creation story, when after creating the world, God rested. But this rest is not because God is tired, John Paul II explains. The Pope envisions God "lingering before the 'very good' work," of creation, especially humans, "in order to cast upon it *a gaze full of joyous delight*. This is a 'contemplative' gaze which does not look to new accomplishments but enjoys the beauty of what has already been achieved."[47] This image calls to mind a parent who delights in watching their child play, or a gardener who rests among her flowers to observe the beauty her work has called forth, enjoying both rest and celebration. Enjoying the beauty of what has already been achieved, contemplating what exists and is real, deeply restores us to our humanness. This restful quality of celebrating is a reason Pieper invokes "feasts"— special times set aside from ordinary work to give thanks for and celebrate what is—as a significant example of times we can experience leisure.

People from the United States are often surprised when they travel abroad and encounter the practices other societies use to protect times of inoperativity for workers. In Europe, travelers may find museums and public sites closed for religious holidays or long lunch breaks. In the holy city of Jerusalem, many Muslim-owned businesses close on Fridays, and not even the buses run during the Jewish Sabbath. When my friend and I missed the last bus home one Friday evening during a trip there, our only choice was to settle in for a long walk. It was a powerful, bodily reminder of how it feels when societies collectively say that efficiency is not the greatest good; bus drivers, too, deserve a day off at the same time as their loved ones.

Jonathan Malesic, the theologian who studied burnout, found that members of Catholic religious orders rarely succumb to burnout, despite busy, productive lives. One protective feature is a structure of life that puts boundaries around the amount of work done, insisting on protecting time for prayer, meals, and leisure even to the extent of giving up income-generating work.[48]

Structures for inoperativity not only protect our own leisure; they remind us that other workers need and deserve leisure too. Part of valuing rest for ourselves is valuing it for others. The detailed instructions given for Sabbath practice in the Hebrew Bible allow human servants, beasts of burden, and even the land itself to rest (*LS'* 68, 71). Pope Francis wrote in *Laudato Si'*: "Rest opens our eyes to the larger picture and gives us renewed sensitivity to the rights of others. And so the day of rest . . . sheds its light on the whole week and motivates us to greater concern for nature and the poor" (*LS'* 237). For Malesic, members of religious orders, with their traditional life balancing work, prayer, and rest, succeed more than many at "living out a belief in each other's dignity."[49] In communities where work productivity is not the highest value, members who grow older or cannot produce the same as others for whatever reason are still valued by others and themselves.

In my own lifetime, one "structure of inoperativity" that used to be fairly common in the United States has started to vanish as more businesses stay open even on major national or religious holidays. When I was a kid in the 1990s, we'd drive past the mall on Christmas on the way to our family celebration. Seeing the darkened signs and the empty parking lots felt strange and special. True, the United States is home to people of many faiths, and there are good reasons not to single out one religious holiday for special treatment. But our secular holidays don't guarantee all workers leisure, either: someone has to staff the Labor Day and July Fourth sales and the "biggest night out" on the day before Thanksgiving. Americans currently have no "structure of inoperativity," no holiday when our desire to take time off to rest and celebrate might extend to allowing others, like bar staff, restaurant servers, and retail workers, to also not be working.

Pieper revealed his own limited perspective by insisting that the one of the highest opportunities for leisure is a feast. Sure—if you're not the one cooking and clearing the plates! Any celebration demands plenty of work: shopping and cooking; readying special outfits, decorations, or music; preparing gifts or a toast. If we are lucky, and part of a family or community that believes in sharing the work, we might find ourselves during the celebration with enough leisure to truly let go and appreciate what is. Or, we could think of a feast in Hinze's terms, as rest-amid. Tomorrow we have to go back to work, and later this evening we'll do the dishes. But right now we get a few moments that refresh us amid our work, moments when our pride in the work and its good outcome give us strength to continue. And hopefully any feast, even if it's rest-amid and not leisure, confirms us in the desire to build the structures that make it possible for other workers to rest and feast, too.

Our personal behavior in our work lives can support structures of inoperativity for ourselves and others. Management experts stress the importance of leaders using sick time, vacation, and parental leave in order to create a workplace culture where employees will feel comfortable doing the same.[50] Anne Helen Petersen, the expert on millennial burnout, introduced readers of her Substack to a message I've had in my email signature ever since: "My working day may not be your working day. Please don't feel obliged to reply to this email outside of your normal working hours."[51] It's important to think seriously about how individual choices can help protect structures of inoperativity for ourselves and others, like this message, which pushes against the sense of unnecessary urgency that sometimes accompanies 24/7 communication technologies. Petersen also points out that personal choices alone won't get us there: unions and labor laws have historically been structures for keeping work's place in our lives manageable, protecting time for leisure.[52] Unions and labor laws still have a very important role to play in creating structures that protect leisure for all workers. One that is increasingly discussed today, in recognition of the fact that many workers are freelance or work for multiple employers throughout a career, is universal basic income.

During the Covid pandemic in 2020, Pope Francis repeatedly called for universal basic income, citing its potential to redress inadequate wages, bring dignity to unpaid work such as caregiving and volunteering, and allow workers time for valuable pursuits beyond paid employment. In April 2020, he addressed a letter to leaders of community movements, writing: "Street vendors, recyclers, carnival workers, small farmers, construction workers, seamstresses, the different kinds of caregivers: you who are informal, working on your own or in the grassroots economy, you have no steady income to get you through this hard time.... This may be the time to consider a universal basic wage which would acknowledge and dignify the noble, essential tasks you carry out."[53] Later that year, the Pope published a book inviting readers to dream toward a better world amid the social upheaval of the pandemic and its lockdowns. Again, he assembled a variety of arguments for basic income, ranging from the practical to the symbolic:

> Recognizing the value to society of the work of non-earners is a vital part of our rethinking in the post-Covid world. That's why I believe it is time to explore concepts like the universal basic income (UBI),... an unconditional flat payment to all citizens, which could be dispersed through the tax system. The UBI could reshape relations in the labor market, guaranteeing people the dignity of refusing employment terms that trap them in poverty. It would give people the basic security they need, remove the stigma of welfarism, and make it easier to move between jobs as technology-driven labor patterns increasingly demand. Policies like the UBI can also help free people to combine earning wages with giving time to the community.[54]

To unpack Francis's thought further, universal basic income grants dignity to those who work without earning wages, as caregivers, community organizers, and more, by providing them with an income. It helps people who work for wages that are inadequate by giving them a supplement to live on and a cushion for exploring better options. Since it is universal, received by everyone in a society, UBI reduces stigma. And since it holds out the possibility of dignified survival without constant waged labor, a UBI can give us time for other pursuits.

All the artists I interviewed spoke of the trade-offs of balancing income-earning labor, creative time, and the downtime that is necessary for creativity. Some independently volunteered that something like a universal basic income would make it much easier for them to balance creating their art with income-earning work and family and other responsibilities. As Andrew Blosser suggests, a universal basic income is indeed a structure for leisure. A highly studied anti-poverty measure, UBI has been pilot-tested in settings as diverse as US states and cities, Canadian provinces, and Native American communities, and countries including Finland, India, Kenya, and Uganda. Overwhelmingly, it is not found to depress participation in the waged workforce, except for students or mothers of young children. It enables people to work less for pay and to spend more time engaged in valuable, productive activities like caregiving, volunteering, or maintaining their homes—which, as we know by now, are also work.[55] UBI is a leisure-promoting structure, but it is not a structure that is antithetical to work.

Conclusion

Pieper believed that people might be immersed in the "world of total work," viewing constant productive activity as life's highest purpose, because they have identified their own personal worth with work or because they have no other choice if they are to survive. In contrast, this chapter highlights the importance of time when we intentionally refrain from productive activity—whether we call this leisure, rest, "doing nothing," or inoperativity—to human well-being, creativity, and flourishing communities. The testimony of working artists affirms that creative activity is, in itself, work, but that leisure is deeply important, not just to the creative work of art-making but for every worker. Adjusting our thinking about work productivity is one solution to the world of total work. For those who have internalized the message that our productivity is our worth, a practice of celebrating what is, including our own selves, is a powerful antidote. For those who are immersed in nothing but work because of financial desperation, different structures are needed. Labor laws can protect time away from paid work, and universal basic income can help people survive voluntary or involuntary times without wages. Practicing leisure should inspire us to work toward a world where all workers have the nonproductive time that is necessary for their well-being, and deserve it not because they work, but because of their human nature.

Notes

1 I refer to "Catholic thought" rather than "Catholic social teaching" in this chapter because the primary Catholic voices are Josef Pieper and

contemporary theologians using his work. Pieper was not a bishop or Pope, in the position to speak authoritatively on behalf of the Church as a whole, but his work reflects a perspective well-informed by the Church tradition and strives to present it accurately and faithfully.

2   Josef Pieper, "The Social Meaning of Leisure in the Modern World," *The Review of Politics* 12, no. 4 (1950): 414.
3   Jon Vickery, "Searching for Josef Pieper," *Theological Studies* 66, no. 3 (September 2005): 622–6.
4   Vickery, "Searching for Josef Pieper," 635–6.
5   Josef Pieper, *No One Could Have Known: An Autobiography: The Early Years, 1904–1945* (San Francisco: Ignatius Press, 1987).
6   Josef Pieper, "Leisure and Its Threefold Opposition (Musse Und Menschliche Existenz)," trans. Lothar Krauth, *Ignatius Insight*, 1963, http://www.ignatiusinsight.com/features2007/jpieper_leisureopp_aug07.asp.
7   Pieper, "Leisure and Its Threefold Opposition."
8   Josef Pieper, *Leisure, the Basis of Culture*, trans. Alexander Dru (San Francisco: Ignatius Press, 2009), 47–48.
9   Christine Firer Hinze, "Presidential Address: Remembering the Rest of Life: Toward a Rest-Inflected Theology of Work and Action," *Proceedings of the Catholic Theological Society of America* 76 (2022): 73.
10 Hinze, "Presidential Address," 73.
11 Hinze, "Presidential Address," 73.
12 Pieper, *Leisure, the Basis of Culture*, 49, 68.
13 Pieper, *Leisure, the Basis of Culture*, 46.
14 Pieper, *Leisure, the Basis of Culture*, 46; Christopher D. Jones and Conor M. Kelly, "Sloth: America's Ironic Structural Vice," *Journal of the Society of Christian Ethics* 37, no. 2 (2017): 117–34, https://doi.org/10.1353/sce.2017.0036.
15 Csikszentmihalyi, *Flow*, 162.
16 Conor M. Kelly, *The Fullness of Free Time: A Theological Account of Leisure and Recreation in the Moral Life* (Washington, DC: Georgetown University Press, 2020), 12–13.
17 Kelly, *The Fullness of Free Time*, 71–8.
18 Csikszentmihalyi, *Flow*, 162.
19 Tricia Hersey, *Rest Is Resistance: A Manifesto* (New York: Little, Brown Spark, 2022), 7.
20 Hersey, *Rest Is Resistance*, 54.
21 Hersey, *Rest Is Resistance*, 85–6.
22 Hersey, *Rest Is Resistance*, 163.

23 Hersey, *Rest Is Resistance*, 62.
24 Hersey, *Rest Is Resistance*, 27.
25 Hersey, *Rest Is Resistance*, 87.
26 Hersey, *Rest Is Resistance*, 171.
27 Jenny Odell, *How to Do Nothing: Resisting the Attention Economy* (Brooklyn, NY: Melville House, 2019), 7.
28 Odell, *How to Do Nothing*, xii.
29 Odell, *How to Do Nothing*, 81.
30 Odell, *How to Do Nothing*, 22.
31 Pieper, "The Social Meaning of Leisure in the Modern World," 415.
32 Enjoying art can be a reliable way to induce a flow experience, although since flow usually relies on the type of engagement that comes through challenge, Csikszentmihalyi believes those who train themselves to appreciate visual art or music are more likely to experience flow when taking it in. *Flow*, 108–9.
33 Anja Notanja Sieger, Personal Interview, May 21, 2024. Sieger's work can be seen at anjanotanja.com.
34 Adebisi Agoro, Personal Interview, May 28, 2024. Agoro's work can be found at blaxlife.com.
35 Nick Garcia, Personal Interview, May 31, 2024. Garcia's music and other projects can be found at bobrokrules.com.
36 Matthew Bailey, Personal Interview, October 30, 2024. Bailey's art is visible at matthewbaileyart.com.
37 Matthew Filipowicz, Personal Interview, May 19, 2024. Filipowicz's comedy and other projects can be seen at matthewf.net.
38 Snežana Žabić, Personal Interview, June 10, 2024. Žabić's work can be found at the press she co-founded, Match Factory Editions, matchfactoryeditions.com.
39 Picture a pie chart divided into three sections, where the key indicates three colors representing "respect," "money" and "so your family will be proud," but those three colors do not appear anywhere in the pie chart.
40 Heidi Parkes, Personal Interview, June 17, 2024. Parkes's work is at heidiparkes.com.
41 Thank you to Kathy Lilla Cox for this generative insight.
42 Hersey, *Rest Is Resistance*, 6.
43 Andrew Blosser, *The Ethics of Doing Nothing: Rest, Rituals, and the Modern World* (Maryknoll, NY: Orbis Books, 2023), 17.
44 Blosser, *The Ethics of Doing Nothing*, 158–63.
45 Blosser, *The Ethics of Doing Nothing*, 130–43.

46 James F. Keenan, "The Liberating Work of Mercy: Banning 'Servile Work,'" *America Magazine*, October 11, 2024, https://www.americamagazine.org/faith/2024/10/11/keenan-works-mercy-servants-248983.

47 John Paul II, "Dies Domini (On Keeping the Lord's Day Holy)," *Vatican.va*, May 31, 1998, para. 11, https://www.vatican.va/content/john-paul-ii/en/apost_letters/1998/documents/hf_jp-ii_apl_05071998_dies-domini.html.

48 Malesic, *The End of Burnout*, 166.

49 Malesic, *The End of Burnout*, 190.

50 Liane Davey, "How to Get Your Team to Use Their Vacation Time," *Harvard Business Review*, August 4, 2017, https://hbr.org/2017/08/how-to-get-your-team-to-use-their-vacation-time.

51 Anne Helen Petersen, "Against 'Feel Free to Take Some Time If You Need It,'" Substack newsletter, *Culture Study* (blog), April 11, 2021, https://annehelen.substack.com/p/against-feel-free-to-take-some-time.

52 Petersen, "Against 'Feel Free to Take Some Time.'"

53 Pope Francis, "Letter of His Holiness Pope Francis to the Popular Movements," *Vatican.va*, April 12, 2020, https://www.vatican.va/content/francesco/en/letters/2020/documents/papa-francesco_20200412_lettera-movimentipopolari.html.

54 Pope Francis and Austen Ivereigh, *Let Us Dream: The Path to a Better Future* (New York: Simon & Schuster, 2020), 131–2. Technically, this book is a statement of Francis's own personal views, not of the Church's tradition via his authority as Pope, and a letter like the one above does not carry the same authority as a document of Church teaching such as an apostolic exhortation or encyclical. However, as we've already seen, the Church's social teaching upholds government support for workers in ways that make UBI a very consistent vision for the tradition.

55 Livia Gershon, "What Happens to Kids When You Give Families a Universal Basic Income?," *JSTOR Daily*, March 27, 2015, https://daily.jstor.org/what-happens-to-kids-when-you-give-families-a-universal-basic-income/; Rebecca Hasdell, "What We Know About Universal Basic Income: A Cross-Synthesis of Reviews," *Stanford Basic Income Lab*, July 2020, https://basicincome.stanford.edu/uploads/Umbrella%20Review%20BI_final.pdf.

6

Making a Living: Just Work and Fair Pay

Chapter Outline

Unjust Working Conditions Today	121
What Could Just Work Look Like?	130
Conclusion	137

It might seem odd to leave discussion of just wages and working conditions until near the end of a book on work. I made that choice to help us focus on Catholic social teaching's inclusive definition of work, which reminds us that work is so much more than paid labor. We've explored the implications of this definition as they relate to how work can harm or restore us, the importance of unpaid work and the need to support it, and the need for time away from paid and unpaid work. That said, just wages and conditions for paid workers are a key way Catholic social teaching sees its view of human dignity being carried out—or not—in the real world. All workers deserve a dignified livelihood and safe, fair working conditions—even if their work is poorly respected or does not generate immediate profit. At the same time, Catholic social teaching does not expect every adult to work for pay, and even calls on communities to offer paths to dignified survival without paid work. Harmful working conditions are not something to be taken for granted, but their causal factors can be understood in order to address and fix them.

Catholic social teaching does not just call on employers and communities to ensure just wages in a general way, but lays out specific plans, adapted to current economic and political circumstances, for how to do so. This chapter will discuss the different models proposed within Catholic social teaching for ensuring every worker receives what they need to live on: the family wage as proposed by Leo XIII and explored by American theologian John A. Ryan; John Paul II's family grants; and the universal basic income advocated by Pope Francis. It will conclude by examining the specific responsibilities of the direct employer; "indirect employers," like governments, whose decisions shape the economy; and workers themselves in shaping a future where every worker enjoys just conditions and compensation.

Some believe that if a worker agreed to a certain wage and conditions, she must be getting a fair deal—if not, why would she agree? Some mainstream economists even teach that everyone is equally free when they enter into the labor market to sell their labor in the way that works best for them.[1] Catholic social teaching sees this view as naïve. Workers routinely agree to conditions and wages that are objectively unfair and even harmful, simply because they need that work to survive. One way of referring to this reality is *economic coercion*. As Daniel Finn explains, "Catholic social thought recognizes that market compulsion can generate injustice in the workplace. This 'force and injustice' not only requires more virtuous action by employers, but, since this is not forthcoming from all employers voluntarily, it also calls for a different structuring of the economy by governmental decision."[2]

Catholic social teaching has long understood that workers are not always equally free to choose to accept or reject wages and conditions. *Rerum Novarum* stated that humans have no right to accept treatment that violates their human dignity, even if they seem to be doing so freely (40): "If the worker, compelled by necessity or by the fear of greater harm, accepts harsher conditions which the employer or contractor impose against the worker's will, this is indeed to undergo force against which justice cries out" (*RN* 45, my translation). Already in 1891, Leo was talking about economic coercion, understanding that the need for survival can act as a kind of force on workers, compelling them, at times, to accept wages and conditions that are below their dignity as human beings. Pointing out economic coercion is not to blame the worker who has little choice but to accept unjust treatment, but to highlight the greater responsibility of employers and government when workers are treated unjustly. Workplace injustice is always wrong, but to correct it, we must understand it in the broader context of the entire economy.

John Paul II also introduced the idea of the *indirect employer* to refer to governments, nonprofit organizations, and others who shape working conditions at the national and international levels (*LE* 18). This helps him explain an idea that goes back to Leo XIII: wages can be unjust, even if the employer is paying the best they can afford, if workers can't survive and support their family on those wages. In such a situation, it may be that a nation's trade policy or historical relationships between nations (such as the aftermath of colonialism) affect the economy in such a way that an employer cannot offer just wages to workers. In this case, the indirect employer—the nation itself, or international agencies or nongovernmental organizations—can and should step in to help.[3] Certainly, sometimes wages or conditions are unjust because of a direct employer's greed or carelessness. But the concept of the indirect employer helps us accurately understand what is going on when, for example, a wildly profitable employer like Amazon offers poor wages or conditions, versus when a small, struggling business does so.

Unjust Working Conditions Today

For Catholic social teaching, unjust working conditions are not just an unfortunate reality, but a serious human rights violation. At Vatican Council II, the world's Catholic bishops used the same Latin term, "probrum," to lament abortion, murder, genocide, slavery, and "disgraceful working conditions, where [workers] are treated as mere tools for profit, rather than as free and responsible persons" (*GS* 27). "Probrum" can mean abuse or disgrace; the official English translation uses "infamy," meaning a violation so bad that it brings public shame on the one who does it. Like genocide, slavery, and the other abuses mentioned, working conditions that treat people as tools for profit "poison human society" and dishonor God (*GS* 27). Because human life is relational, no one harms a person without harming their community as well, and this is still true when the harm takes place in a paid workplace.

Sometimes, a single employer chooses on their own to pay poorly or to mistreat workers. More often, exploitative working conditions result from the indirect employer as much as the direct one—from market conditions shaped by governments, by the choices of millions of consumers, and by the forces of history. This does not mean we must accept them, but we must understand them rightly when working toward safer, fairly paid jobs.

The fact that indirect employers shape working conditions means we do not accept "what the market will bear" to justify inadequate wages or unsafe conditions. "The market" does not exist in a vacuum but is shaped by human choices throughout history. For example, extreme inequality between wealthier countries and poorer ones, which are often former colonizing powers and the nations they dominated, remains a sad reality that shapes working conditions around the world. *Populorum Progressio* (1967), an encyclical on international development, observed that due to this history of domination, poorer nations and wealthier ones do not compete on an equal playing field when it comes to trade agreements. Agreements between nations cannot be considered just simply because both parties agree to them, but must be for the genuine benefit of both sides, offering just, family-supporting jobs to workers in poorer areas (*PP* 59–61). John Paul II called upon wealthier countries to "lighten, defer or even cancel" the debts of poorer nations so that their citizens would not suffer because of debts contracted by their governments (*CA* 35).

Inequality between countries is often responsible for dangerous working conditions in poorer nations, as Pope Benedict XVI pointed out. To attract businesses that sell goods to wealthy countries, the governments of poorer nations may limit legal protections for workers or cut social safety nets (*CV* 25). This means that in many poorer countries, working conditions that would be unthinkable in richer nations are still common. For example, fatal construction accidents are a daily news item in India, where employers rarely follow safety precautions and no government agency bears responsibility for ensuring they do.[4] Globally, 160 million children engage in child labor, which the United Nations defines as work that threatens to harm child workers physically or mentally or to disrupt their education.[5] Plastic trash from wealthy countries is exported to poorer ones for sorting by workers who risk exposure to toxic chemicals with no regulatory protection or legal recourse.[6] Responsibility for these harmful working conditions lies with the international companies that seek labor at the lowest price without taking into account worker safety in the locations where they hire. Pope Francis condemned the "globalization of indifference" that lets citizens of wealthy countries enjoy their luxuries while many throughout the world experience dire poverty, as well as the "magic theories" that claim increased wealth at the top will trickle down and benefit the poor, without real-world evidence of this happening (*EG* 54). He observed that when inequality grows along with wealth, "new forms of poverty" emerge: for example, while access to electricity was once considered a luxury, now it may be considered necessary in order to live and work with dignity (*FT* 125–6). Climate change impacts millions of workers who work outside or in poorly climate-controlled environments, where heat can literally lead to death on the job. Despite climate change contributing to increasing temperatures, some direct and indirect employers—large businesses and US states that want to cater to business—are opposing improved safety measures for workers.[7]

Migration has always been part of the reality of human work, but today's vast inequalities between nations bring distinct challenges for workers who attempt it. In 1967, Pope Paul VI called for a "warm welcome" for migrant workers along with efforts to build shared prosperity in poorer countries, allowing their citizens to become leaders in developing stable and flourishing economic environments at home (*PP* 65, 69, 70). Migrating for better opportunities is not without trade-offs, Pope Benedict XVI reminds us, making it more difficult to form stable life commitments such as marriage (*CV* 25). Pope Francis summed up the complexity of the Church's tradition on migration when he wrote:

> Ideally, unnecessary migration ought to be avoided; this entails creating in countries of origin the conditions needed for a dignified life and integral development. Yet until substantial progress is made in achieving this goal, we are obliged to respect the right of all individuals to find a place that meets their basic needs and those of their families, and where they can find personal fulfilment. Our response to the arrival of migrating persons can be summarized by four words: welcome, protect, promote and integrate. (*FT* 129)

Francis called for significant legal rights for migrants, including safe housing, employment, and integration into the local community, and "*full citizenship* . . . for those who are not recent arrivals and already participate in the fabric of society" (*FT* 131). In a co-authored public letter, the Catholic bishops of Mexico and the United States observed that a path to legal status is necessary to protect migrants' human rights because unscrupulous employers will use workers' insecure legal status to exploit them. Even those who enter a country without the permission of its government must retain their human rights.[8]

The Catholic tradition recognizes that often people migrate because conditions at home are unworthy of human dignity, such as dangerous conflict or an inability to afford food, shelter, and survival. "No one leaves home unless home is the mouth of a shark," as the British-Somali poet Warsan Shire wrote about the refugee experience.[9] The right to migrate exists hand in hand with the right to find safety and opportunity in one's own home. Still, the fact that a person migrates does nothing to change the basic fact of their human dignity and the rights and considerations that are due to them, as workers and as people, from the community where they end up. The Church knows that workers who migrate often end up marginalized in the receiving society, facing unjust treatment and poor wages due to their vulnerable status. From a Catholic perspective, this is completely unacceptable.

Evolving technology brings great opportunities as well as new challenges to worker dignity. The great connectivity of the Internet is stewarded by anonymous data workers who provide human analysis of user-submitted content. Global media companies seek out workers with good English skills who lack the legal protections of the wealthier nations where those companies are based. For example, content moderators and data annotators in countries including Kenya and Uganda manage user-submitted content that is frequently violent, hateful, or traumatizing. Media companies' desire to protect end users from such content requires the human data workers to engage with it constantly, closely evaluating graphic videos depicting fatal car crashes, beheadings, suicide, and rape.[10] In wealthier economies, technology expands the ways employers can control the movements workers make and the targets they must meet. The retail behemoth Amazon uses high-tech surveillance software to monitor everything from warehouse workers' packing speed, to their adherence to Covid safety protocols, to their unionization efforts.[11]

Work that treats the person as a cog in a machine, or exposes them repeatedly to traumatic material, is obviously profoundly alienating, as *Laborem Exercens* describes work that harms "the workers' physical health or . . . their moral integrity" (*LE* 19). Jobs that harm moral integrity are not limited to traumatizing data work. When workers have the skills to do important work but lack the resources to do it well, they can suffer *moral injury*, a term for the harm caused when people view themselves as morally damaged because they participated in or failed to prevent something that goes against their moral beliefs. At work, moral injury can happen when workers are expected to participate in harm to others, to violate their own or formal workplace ethical codes, or when they do not have the resources necessary to do their job well, resulting in harm to those they serve. For example, when nurses are assigned to care for too many patients at once, they may suffer knowing that they are not giving each patient quality care, just as educators do when they are unable to give each student the time and resources they need to learn.[12] Work that causes moral injury due to a lack of needed resources would not have to be alienating in different conditions. Catholic social teaching would call on direct and indirect employers to make sure workers have the resources needed to do their jobs with integrity.

Catholic social teaching has been concerned about work's moral impact on the workers long before psychiatrist Jonathan Shay coined the term "moral injury" in the 1990s. In 1931, Pius XI wrote about the harmful moral impact of being treated not as a human, but as a tool. Reflecting on how common it seemed to be for paid work to harm people in this way, he concluded, "Inanimate material comes out of the factory greatly improved, but people are corrupted and made worse there" (*QA* 135, my translation). Working conditions that "corrupt" factory workers are not intrinsic to the work; Pius blames them on the greed of employers, which government intervention could prevent (*QA* 132–4).

Another "violation of the dignity of human work" is the lack of work for those who need it (*CV* 63). It is a problem when people can't support themselves and their families through work, whether because paid work is not available, because the work available doesn't pay enough to live on, or they lack necessary resources for the work they can do, such as when farmers lose their land. As we saw, Catholic social teaching supports workers receiving a livelihood from the community through the government if they are unable to earn one on their own. However, the tradition recognizes that "ordinarily" or "in the majority of cases" people meet their basic needs through work (*GS* 67, *MM* 18). CST framers carefully avoid stigmatizing those who cannot support themselves through work, which may be a relatively uncommon situation, but is not immoral or something to be judged. Another example of this is John Paul II's "the family needs the necessities of life which humans customarily gain for themselves through work" (*LE* 10, my translation). But the tradition recognizes that most people would prefer to access their basic needs through work, both because of all the benefits work brings to the person and because they may well have no other option. The lack of work that allows people to support themselves and their families is a serious violation of human dignity.

Unemployment and underemployment "demonstrate that both within the individual political communities, and in their relationships on the continental and world level there is something wrong with the organization of work and employment" (*SRS* 18). Pope Francis wrote that lack of work leaves people "excluded and marginalized... without any means of escape" (*Evangelii Gaudium* 53). In his public speeches as well as his formal teaching on behalf of the Church, Francis often mentioned the human right to *tierra, techo y trabajo*, in his native Spanish, or land, housing, and work (*FT* 127). This slogan, which social justice movements in Latin America have adopted, shows the complexity of obtaining basic needs and the responsibility of indirect employers to create the conditions for people to meet them.[13] Someone might have work but still be unable to afford housing or other necessities of life because of unjust wages (more on this all-too-common situation later). If farmers can't sell their produce at a price that supports their basic needs, having land and being able to farm it still may not keep them housed. This shows how complex unemployment and underemployment are, not to be solved with a simplistic approach of "add waged work and stir." Indirect employers, especially government, are in the best position to balance all the complexities of pursuing the goal of family-supporting work for everyone who needs it.

Some assume that problems like poverty, hunger, homelessness, lack of access to health care, and more would be solved if needy people would just "get a job." This "add waged work and stir" approach ignores the fact that some people are unable to work because of health conditions or other responsibilities, such as family members who need care. It also ignores the more serious problem of unjust compensation for paid work, which means that many people living in poverty, without stable access to housing or food, or lacking health care, are in fact working for pay. Some are working multiple jobs without being able to afford the necessities of life—and this is by no means an uncommon situation.

The nonprofit United Way reports that 42 percent of US households are unable to afford basic survival needs. They estimated the cost of a basic "survival budget" including rent, food, child care, transportation, health insurance premiums, taxes, a smartphone for every adult in the family, and a small amount for other expenses, not including savings.[14] Of the households unable to afford these basic necessities, 13 percent have incomes below the federal poverty level, and the remaining 29 percent belong to a group the United Way calls ALICE—Asset Limited, Income Constrained, Employed. A family whose income is above the federal poverty level is likely to have at least one person working one job, if not more—but this employment is no guarantee that the family will be able to afford their basic needs. In 2021, 52.5 million US households fell below the ALICE threshold for meeting basic needs—nearly half of the households in the country. Wages that do not provide a dignified human standard of living are a "grave injustice" (*Compendium* 302). We should not accept this injustice just because it is so sadly common in the United States.

Most advocates agree that the federal poverty level does not represent a basic standard of living but a benchmark far below that, a criticism the US government seems to recognize when it extends certain forms of assistance, like health care subsidies, to those earning multiples of the federal poverty level income. Still, even at the very low incomes captured by the federal poverty level, we can find many people working. While those whose incomes fall below the federal poverty level are "primarily adults who had not participated in the labor force during the year and children, 6.3 million individuals were among the 'working poor' in 2020."[15] The fact that so many children live below a very inadequate income standard in the United States is a scandal of its own, made worse by the fact that often, they suffer this poverty despite the fact that their parents are working. In 2017, the most recent year family-specific data are available, 24.1 percent of single-parent families lived below the federal poverty level. Of these, 18.4 percent of the parents worked full time, meaning over 2.3 million families had a parent in the full-time workforce and could not meet even the very inadequate federal poverty level.[16] Catholic social teaching insists that everyone has a right to their basic needs—this right does not depend on working. But even those not committed to the Catholic understanding of human rights ought to agree that if someone cannot meet their basic needs while working full time, an injustice is occurring. Wages inadequate to human dignity are a shamefully common reality in the United States.

For those who are working and still fall below the federal poverty level, the most common occupational groups are service (8% of the working poor) and farming, fishing, and forestry (10%).[17] The ALICE group, which contains households that are above the federal poverty level but still not meeting basic needs, includes almost 70 percent of janitors; more than half of home health aides; nearly half of cashiers, food service workers, and restaurant waitstaff; and more than a fourth of retail salespeople, stockers, and truck drivers.[18] In other words, almost half of US people who are working without making ends meet are doing work that the rest of us rely on in our daily lives. Nor are such low-paid jobs a "stepping stone" to better working conditions—researchers found that they are "all too often poverty traps," where workers experience difficulty moving on to better employment.[19] The injustice of their wages does not only matter to these workers. If we shop in stores or eat in restaurants, we are supporting the employers who underpay them, and this injustice should matter to all of us.

Haven't there always been poorly paid jobs at the lower end of the income spectrum? The conservative think tank American Compass bluntly states, "While many economists argue that America's working families are more prosperous than ever before, families themselves feel that they have come under increasing economic pressure. The families are right."[20] American Compass created the Cost-of-Thriving Index (CoTI), attempting to compare the ability of wages to secure the goods needed for life as they are priced and available in the time in question—in other words, what it means to earn a "middle-class living" in 2022 vs. 1985. CoTI calculates the number of working weeks it would take one worker to pay for housing, health care, food, education, and transportation—the basic dignities of a middle-class life for many Americans.[21] In 1985, men who had graduated high school could afford this list of goods in less than forty-five weeks of work, meaning, assuming they worked a full year, they would be able to spend on luxuries or save for emergencies. In 2020, the only demographic group that could afford CoTI in less than fifty-two work weeks was men who had completed college. The groups including all US men, all US women, or men who had completed high school would have to work more than fifty-two weeks in a year to be able to afford this standard—in other words, those basic measures of a thriving life, which a high school-educated man could afford in 1985, are out of reach for those groups today. Concludes American Compass founder Oren Cass, "One might debate what set of costs a middle-class family *should* be able to afford, but it is indisputable that the set used in CoTI is one that a middle-class family *could* afford a generation ago on one income and *cannot* afford any longer without having two incomes or significant government support."[22]

Precarious work is not limited to workers who fall below the poverty level or those in the better-off, but still struggling group described as ALICE. In the United States, a "pronounced risk shift from employers to employees" has taken place since the 1970s, as workers have experienced increased job insecurity and diminished access to employer benefits such as health care and retirement. "Precarity is complex and multifaceted, but key dimensions include low and stagnant wages and rising uncertainty about the amount and timing of work hours employers will offer from one week to the next," the researchers note.[23] The consequences of this instability and diminished access to benefits are seen in increased rates of disability, severe illness, and early death, especially among working-class and less educated workers.[24] One example of the risk shift from employers onto low-wage workers is the rise of "just-in-time scheduling," in which workers are expected to be constantly available for a work schedule that is always subject to change. This maximizes employer profits by limiting the amount of time worksites may have more staff than strictly necessary but imposes significant costs on workers, increasing psychological distress and unhappiness and harming sleep quality, particularly because of the ways work and the rest of life are often thrown into conflict by an unpredictable work schedule.[25] Maximizing profits through policies that endanger workers' physical and mental health and shorten their lifespan clearly values property over human life in ways that Catholic social teaching labels as immoral.

The contemporary situation of families needing to maintain two full-time workers in order to sustain a middle-class lifestyle was explored by Elizabeth Warren and Amelia Warren Tyagi in their book *The Two-Income Trap*, first published in 2003. For Warren and Tyagi, the influx of women into the paid workforce—despite the many real reasons to celebrate this change—inadvertently concealed that economic circumstances were less favorable to middle-class and poor families than in the past. While during the postwar period, families could comfortably survive on one income while affording stable housing and education (as explained above), through the 1970s and beyond, many families found that they needed both parents to be working in order to secure those goods. This meant, Warren and Tyagi point out, that those families are ultimately less financially secure because they have less to fall back on. "For middle-class families, the most important part of the safety net for generations has been the stay-at-home mother," whose labor power functioned as insurance to be tapped if the male breadwinner lost his job or ability to work.[26] "A stay-at-home mother functioned as the family's ultimate insurance against unemployment or disability—insurance that had a very real economic value even when it wasn't drawn on."[27] Warren and Tyagi observe that the two-income trap emerged because both conservatives who urged women to stay home and feminists who exhorted them into the workforce "discounted the financial value of the stay-at-home mother."[28]

Opposition to labor unions is a major condition threatening just employment. This is not only because unions tend to be an effective way for workers to win better wages and safer conditions, but because "the right of association is a natural right of the human being" (*CA* 7). When employers try to stop workers from forming unions, they are not just holding those workers back in their fight for better conditions, but denying a part of their basic humanity. Humans are social and need relationships with others to thrive. Joining with coworkers to improve conditions at work is a natural expression of our humanity. Unions "serve the development of an authentic culture of work and help workers to share in a fully human way in the life of their place of employment" (*CA* 15). People sometimes think that unions are no longer needed in well-paying professions or countries with strong worker safety laws. But because unions express and honor people's social nature as well as help them defend their rights at work, Benedict XVI insisted that the Church's calls for supporting the creation of strong unions "must be honored today even more than in the past" (*CV* 25).

What Could Just Work Look Like?

Framers of Catholic social teaching usually claim that the tradition does not have a specific policy agenda: for example, Benedict XVI wrote that "the Church does not have technical solutions to offer . . .

[but] does, however, have a mission of truth to accomplish" (*CV* 10). At the beginning of this book, I insisted that Catholic social teaching is a fully developed worldview, not just a set of policy proposals. However, within the documents of Catholic social teaching we do find, not only general statements of the truth of human dignity, but also fairly specific recommendations for the policies societies should adopt to support it. Such policies are not dreamed up by the Popes themselves but reflect consultation with experts in economics, development, public policy, and other social sciences. These recommendations reflect the best understanding available of concerns at the times when they are written, meaning that, unlike the consistent vision of human dignity, they evolve with the times. Catholic social teaching has consistently held that the responsibility for providing safe and justly paid work does not belong to employers alone but is shared by a whole community, represented by the government. The distinct policies the Church has proposed in support of this vision are all rooted in the same basic convictions: that every worker, whether employed for pay or not, deserves the resources they need to live in dignity, and wages must take into account that many workers support people besides themselves. I'll discuss specific proposals and how they've evolved while comparing them with on-the-ground realities for worker compensation in the United States.

The oldest specific wage policy called for in Catholic social teaching is a family wage. In *Rerum Novarum*, Leo XIII insisted that pay must follow "the dictate of natural justice" and be enough to support a "frugal and well behaved wage earner" and "his wife and his children" (*RN* 45-6). A fair wage is not just what the market will bear, and the Church desires unpaid workers to have what they need to survive, just as much as paid workers. The family wage proposal also respects the human nature of the wage-earning worker, who is not an isolated individual but a social and relational human being who may have loved ones to provide for. The call for a family wage is not just a way to make sure children and unpaid caregivers can survive—it's an expression of the truth that workers are human and humans are relational.

In the United States during the first half of the twentieth century, the priest and economist John A. Ryan applied *Rerum Novarum*'s teachings to calculate a family wage in dollars and advocate for it as public policy. A living wage was not the bare survival minimum, but would allow the worker to afford "food, clothing, shelter, insurance, and mental and spiritual culture—all in a reasonable degree" for himself and his family.²⁹ Like Leo XIII, Ryan presumed that most families would be supported through the wages of a male breadwinner, although he was familiar with women working for pay in the US context and believed working women had a right to an individual living wage.³⁰ A family wage for male breadwinners was not simply a convenient means of ensuring support for children, but something that went along with the human dignity of the worker; as he is a relational person who has the right to found a family, his employer and community have the duty to ensure that his work can support that family in their needs.³¹ Ryan advocated laws requiring a family-supporting wage but believed unionization would also help achieve it.³²

Ryan's living wage, which took into account the needs of workers' particular families, is different from the vision of living wage movements today. Still, Catholic organizations have often supported modern "living wage" movements, understanding that they move communities closer to the goal of just wages. These movements often understand a living wage as one that allows a worker (and sometimes the family they support) to live with dignity without needing any public assistance. Some "living wage" movements define it in terms of a dollar amount, such as the Fight for $15 (an hour) movement in the United States. Others advocate for a revisable living wage that would undergo regular cost-of-living updates.³³ These movements obviously share significant concerns with Catholic social teaching, such as the concern that wages be determined via reference to a worker's needs, not by what the market will bear. For the sake of clarity, the demands of "living wage" movements are not identical to the vision of Catholic social teaching, which takes into account what businesses can afford to pay when evaluating wage justice (*MM* 71). Living wage movements are effective at raising living standards for workers in a certain area and at forcing profitable employers to pay workers what they deserve rather than simply what the market will bear, all of which Catholic social teaching applauds. However, if a successful living wage movement drove the legal minimum wage high enough that certain small businesses were no longer able to afford to pay their employees, Catholic social teaching would regard that as regrettable. Of course, as theologian Dan Finn writes, "Acknowledging that any particular firm may be unable to pay a just wage does not dissolve the indictment of our economic system. It presses us to do more to rectify the injustice."³⁴ If small businesses can't afford to pay workers living wages, the community might step in with subsidies to those businesses or assistance to their workers.

When early Catholic social teaching envisioned a just wage as a wage on which one worker can support a family, the documents put it in plainly gendered terms: men must be paid wages that allow them to support a family so wives do not need to work for wages and can focus on caring for children (e.g., *RN* 42, *QA* 71). Of course, the very fact that the same documents lamented women and children working for wages shows that the vision of a single male breadwinner was never attainable for many families. Another factor to keep in mind is that safe child care facilities were not available to most workers during the time of Leo XIII and Pius XI, as they are not for many poorer workers now. Industrial Revolution-era parents might bring babies into the factories or leave them home with an older sibling, neither option ideal for children's safe and healthy development.

Certainly, historical gender ideology contributes to early CST's depiction of a family wage supporting a male breadwinner and a female homemaker, but the policy is also an attempt to guarantee support for unpaid care labor at a community-wide level and an acknowledgment that such work is important to the whole society. As Christine Firer Hinze put it, "Within an industrialized money economy, economic support for families has been envisaged by the popes as normally requiring the work of two adults," a wage earner and an unpaid worker focusing on the home and family.[35] Contrast this vision with the economic status quo, which often requires all adults in a family to work for wages in order to make ends meet, or US "welfare reform," which pushes mothers of young children into the paid workforce instead of allowing them to survive as at-home caregivers, as the US welfare system was initially intended to do.[36] Following the "welfare reform" of the late 1990s, nearly half of US states require a newborn's parent to be working or looking for work for at least twenty hours a week by the time the baby is three months old in order to receive cash assistance. Only two states will provide cash assistance to parents of children older than a year.[37] CST has always disagreed with the ideas advanced along with US welfare reform: that paid work grants dignity in a way unpaid work does not; that caring for one's own child is neither work nor dignifying; and that people who are not engaged in paid work do not deserve to have their basic needs met.

The economic status quo, and welfare reform, do not treat unpaid family care as work worthy of support. Early CST's family wage, for all of its dated gender ideology, does. The tradition does not shame women (or children) who went to work for wages when their families had no other choice, but condemns direct and indirect employers for not offering wages on which one worker can support a family. As education access expanded throughout the globe and other options made it clear that children could be cared for safely without a mother needing to stay home, Catholic social teaching changed in response. Contemporary documents no longer call explicitly for work to allow mothers to stay home but for the total economic environment to support a mother's—and recently also the father's—important role in raising children (*LE* 19, *AL* 55).

What has not changed is the tradition's consistent insistence that unpaid care is work that deserves to be compensated, whether this is done through the caregiver's spouse earning a family-supporting wage or through the government supporting caregivers on behalf of the community. In 1981, John Paul II was willing to see the goal of supporting dependent persons and unpaid workers met, either by employers paying a "family wage," or the government providing "family allowances or grants to mothers devoting themselves exclusively to their families" (*LE* 19). This contemporary update to the ideal of a family-supporting wage showed the understanding that the community as a whole should contribute to families' livelihoods, especially in cases where a single worker's wages are inadequate or, potentially, for single parents who would prefer to remain caregivers. This vision is aligned with the way many developed economies have chosen to support families in the latter half of the twentieth century. Making grants directly to parents is simpler than trying to enforce a system where each private business must pay different wages to sole breadwinners with families of different sizes.

When government family grants are discussed in the United States, some argue that government should use them to reward or discourage particular models of family formation and support. For example, some argue that government benefits should level off after a family has a certain number of children, the so-called "family cap," which punishes larger families who receive public assistance. Others argue for "promoting marriage" by limiting supports only to families where the parents are married. As researcher Amber Lapp points out, limiting support for families only to those families who look a certain way punishes those families who may be among the most vulnerable, not to mention the children of those families, who had no say in the family's configuration.[38] These types of social engineering manipulations are not part of the Church's vision for government support of families. Of course, a child does not cease to have human dignity because she's being raised by her grandparents, and a caregiver's work still deserves compensation if he is an unmarried single dad. Family grants, or other support for workers, are the right of everyone on the basis of their human dignity and relational nature, not a tool for governments to use for social engineering. And supporting families is in and of itself good for society because society is made up of families of all different shapes and sizes. As John Paul II wrote, "In the conviction that the good of the family is an indispensable and essential value of the civil community, the public authorities must do everything possible to ensure that families have all those aids—economic, social, educational, political and cultural assistance—that they need in order to face all their responsibilities in a human way" (*FC* 45).

Perhaps trying to stave off such attempts to limit government assistance only to particular families, the Pontifical Council for Justice and Peace clearly specified in 2004: "There can be several different ways to make a family wage a concrete reality. Various forms of important social provisions help to bring it about, for example, family subsidies and other contributions for dependent family members, and also remuneration for the domestic work done in the home by one of the parents" (*Compendium* 250). Whatever the gender or age of the caregiver providing it, caregiving work in the home deserves "economic compensation in keeping with that of other types of work" (251).

The idea that everyone deserves to have their basic needs met, whether they work for pay or not, has gained public traction in recent years with discussions of the basic income guarantee. Under this policy, the government would provide everyone with a basic survival income in cash, funded through taxes. For example, around $10,000 a year, plus guaranteed health care, has been suggested as a basic income for the US. Pope Francis has said that guaranteeing compensation to unpaid caregivers through a universal basic income would help societies "move beyond this idea that the work of the caregiver for her relative, or a full-time mother or volunteer in a social project, is not work because it pays no wages."[39] Unpaid work provides significant benefits to communities, he notes; basic income would compensate unpaid workers for the many ways they contribute to the common good.[40] This is again a contemporary vision of an idea first advocated in the form of a family wage; communities should guarantee that even those who don't work for pay can reliably access basic needs.

As is clear by now, Catholic social teaching has never envisioned a world where all adults work outside the home for wages. Try half of that amount: the tradition has historically hoped that half the adults in a society would be able to devote themselves to the unpaid labor of caring for family, maintaining the home, and building up the community. While we rightly reject the earlier assumption that unpaid home caregivers would all be women, it's important not to lose the much more radical point that the Catholic tradition has never imagined waged work as a requirement for all adults. And the tradition has never understood waged work as the only way to attain our basic human needs, as we can clearly see by the fact that it elevates a vision of an economy where fully half of adults can spend their time in important, unwaged work, deriving their support and basic needs from a partner who earns a family wage, from society supporting them via the government, or both.

Catholic social teaching sees just compensation for paid work as providing stability and security for the worker and their family while they are working and into the future. Leo XIII called for wages high enough to allow workers to support a family and build savings. The ability to save and acquire property through waged work would allow ordinary working people to move toward self-sufficiency and a stable future (*RN* 46). Property could provide "a modest source of income" that would be a worker's only way to retire in the days before governments offered safety nets and strong unions won retirement guarantees. "The Catholic social tradition acknowledges that an important aspect of ownership is that it enables persons to plan and make decisions about their future," exercising their God-given responsibility and freedom, theologian James Bailey explains.[41] Leo's vision is similar to what modern anti-poverty organizations call "asset building" approaches. In order to climb out of poverty, people not only need a decent income; they also need savings that they can use to weather hard times or to invest in education, a home, a business, or other sources of economic stability.[42] This vision—that a just wage is not just survival, but the ability to save and accumulate stability for the future—has been part of Catholic social teaching since it began.

More recent encyclicals added detail to the list of benefits that are the right of paid and unpaid workers alike. Along with family-supporting wages, workers deserve low-cost or free health care; a retirement pension and insurance in case they are no longer able to work; maternity leave; and working conditions that are safe for body and soul (*LE* 19, *Compendium* 301). They have the right to weekly rest and yearly vacations. In the United States today, this package of benefits would be seen as fairly generous, likely available to only the most in-demand workers. (Only 24% of US workers can access paid family leave; for those who get their health care coverage through work, benefits increasingly cover less and less real care, and with higher out of pocket costs.[43]) For Catholic social teaching, they are the right of every worker, whose human nature demands time for rest and relational connection.

Conclusion

This chapter discussed unjust working conditions that continue to persist in our world today, including jobs that expose workers to moral injury; discriminatory treatment of migrants; the lack of work for those who want it; and wages that do not allow a family, or even a single worker, to afford their basic needs. Catholic social teaching would regard these injustices as the responsibility of direct employers and also of indirect employers, larger entities capable of shaping the economic environment where work takes place, such as governments. The CST tradition has put forth many concrete policies for ensuring worker justice, including a "family wage" that allows one breadwinner to support dependents; "family grants" where the government compensates unpaid caregivers; and universal basic income. While these proposals were at times framed in ways that limited the roles of both men and women, they all share a commitment to ensuring people can access basic needs even if they are not currently working for pay, and to recognizing that unpaid caregiving work is important to the flourishing of families and communities.

The CST tradition does not specify whether the employer or the government should bear the cost of these rights for workers; its vision for just work and fair pay sees this goal as everyone's responsibility. While the government should take a strong and active role in securing workers' rights, direct employers have obvious responsibilities, and workers themselves can take the lead in fighting for just working conditions. The final chapter offers more concrete detail about what the government, direct employers, and workers themselves can do to move toward just work and fair compensation for every worker.

Notes

1. E.g. *Free To Choose: The Power of the Market*, vol. 1, Free to Choose, 1980, http://freetochoosenetwork.org/programs/free_to_choose/. Economist Milton Friedman suggests in this video, which aired on national television, that workers seen laboring in sweatshop conditions must have freely accepted those conditions as a trade-off for higher wages.
2. Finn, *Christian Economic Ethics*, 247.
3. Donal Dorr, *Option for the Poor: A Hundred Years of Vatican Social Teaching*, Rev. ed. (Maryknoll, NY: Orbis Books, 1992), 292.
4. Zachary Phillips, "Construction Had the Most Fatalities of Any Industry Last Year," *Construction Dive*, December 19, 2023, https://www.constructiondive.com/news/construction-fatalities-2023-bls-falls-safety/702974/; Mateen Hafeez, Swati Deshpande, and Chittaranjan Tembhekar, "In Three Years, Three-Fold Rise in Deaths of Construction Workers in Maharashtra," *The Times of India*, September 12, 2023, https://timesofindia.indiatimes.com/city/mumbai/in-three-years-three-fold-rise-in-deaths-of-construction-workers/articleshow/103591477.cms.
5. n.a., "Child Labor," UN Special Representative of the Secretary-General on Violence Against Children, n.d., https://violenceagainstchildren.un.org/content/Child%20Labour.
6. Erin McCormick et al., "Where Does Your Plastic Go? Global Investigation Reveals America's Dirty Secret," *The Guardian*, June 17, 2019, https://www.theguardian.com/us-news/2019/jun/17/recycled-plastic-america-global-crisis.
7. Whizy Kim, "This Summer Is Giving Us a Glimpse at the Dangerous Future of Work," *Vox*, August 25, 2023, https://www.vox.com/23844420/extreme-heat-work-labor-osha-climate-change.
8. United States Conference of Catholic Bishops and Conferencia del Episcopado Mexicano, "Strangers No Longer: Together on the Journey of Hope," *USCCB*, January 22, 2003, 74–75, https://www.usccb.org/

9. Warsan Shire, "Conversations About Home (At the Deportation Centre)," from *teaching my mother how to give birth* (flipped eye, London, 2013), available at Poetry International, https://www.poetryinternational.com/en/poets-poems/poems/poem/103-22840_CONVERSATIONS-ABOUT-HOME-AT-THE-DEPORTATION-CENTRE#lang-org

10. Callum Cant, James Muldoon, and Mark Graham, *Feeding the Machine: The Hidden Human Labor Powering A.I.* (New York: Bloomsbury Publishing, 2024), 2.

11. Cant, Muldoon, and Graham, *Feeding the Machine*, 121.

12. Ron Carucci and Ludmila N. Praslova, "Employees Are Sick of Being Asked to Make Moral Compromises," *Harvard Business Review*, February 21, 2022, https://hbr.org/2022/02/employees-are-sick-of-being-asked-to-make-moral-compromises; Victoria Williamson, Sharon A. M. Stevelink, and Neil Greenberg, "Occupational Moral Injury and Mental Health: Systematic Review and Meta-Analysis," *The British Journal of Psychiatry: The Journal of Mental Science* 212, no. 6 (June 2018): 339–46, https://doi.org/10.1192/bjp.2018.55.

13. Kevin Clarke, "Pope Francis Wants You to Remember the Three T's: Tierra, Techo, Trabajo (Land, Lodging, Labor)," *America Magazine*, October 22, 2021, https://www.americamagazine.org/politics-society/2021/10/22/pope-francis-tierra-trabajo-techo-slogan-241699.

14. Stephanie Hoopes et al., "ALICE in the Crosscurrents: Covid and Financial Hardship in the United States," *UnitedForAlice.org*, April 2023, 3, https://www.unitedforalice.org/Attachments/AllReports/23UFA_Report_National_4.11.23_FINAL.pdf.

15. n.a., "A Profile of the Working Poor, 2020," *Bureau of Labor Statistics*, September 2022, https://www.bls.gov/opub/reports/working-poor/2020/.

16. Timothy Grall, "Custodial Mothers and Fathers and Their Child Support: 2017," *Census.gov*, May 2020, https://www.census.gov/content/dam/Census/library/publications/2020/demo/p60-269.pdf.

17. n.a., "A Profile of the Working Poor, 2020."

18. Hoopes et al., "ALICE in the Crosscurrents," 14.

19. Robert O'Neill, "Are 'Bad Jobs' Dead Ends or Steppingstones to Better Things? New Research Identifies Some Pathways to Better Job Quality," *Harvard Kennedy School*, August 7, 2024, https://www.hks.harvard.edu/

faculty-research/policy-topics/social-policy/are-bad-jobs-dead-ends-or-steppingstones-better-things.
20 Oren Cass, "2023 Cost-of-Thriving Index," *American Compass*, February 14, 2023, https://americancompass.org/2023-cost-of-thriving-index/.
21 These goods are defined in ways that can be consistently measured across decades: for example, federal estimates of average costs for food and housing, or the cost of in-state tuition and fees at a public college for educational costs.
22 Cass, "2023 Cost-of-Thriving Index."
23 Schneider and Harknett, "Work-Schedule Instability."
24 Schneider and Harknett, "Work-Schedule Instability."
25 Schneider and Harknett, "Work-Schedule Instability."
26 Elizabeth Warren and Amelia Warren Tyagi, *The Two-Income Trap: Why Middle-Class Parents Are Going Broke*, Reprint ed. (New York: Basic Books, 2004), 56.
27 Warren and Tyagi, *The Two-Income Trap*, 59.
28 Warren and Tyagi, *The Two-Income Trap*, 67.
29 Quoted in Christine Firer Hinze, "Bridge Discourse on Wage Justice: Roman Catholic and Feminist Perspectives on the Family Living Wage," *Annual of the Society of Christian Ethics*, January 1, 1991, 113.
30 Christine Firer Hinze, *Radical Sufficiency: Work, Livelihood, and a US Catholic Economic Ethic* (Washington, D.C.: Georgetown University Press, 2021), 38.
31 Hinze, *Radical Sufficiency*, 38.
32 Hinze, *Radical Sufficiency*, 40.
33 Victoria Masterson, "Explainer: What Is a Living Wage and How Is It Different from the Minimum Wage?," *World Economic Forum*, April 9, 2024, https://www.weforum.org/stories/2024/04/ilo-living-wage-explained/.
34 Finn, *Christian Economic Ethics*, 248.
35 Hinze, "Legacy," 78.
36 Robert A. Moffitt, "The Deserving Poor, the Family, and the U.S. Welfare System," *Demography* 52, no. 3 (June 2015): 729–49, https://doi.org/10.1007/s13524-015-0395-0.
37 Hahn et al., "Work Requirements," 7.
38 Lapp, "Child Benefit."
39 Pope Francis and Austen Ivereigh, *Let Us Dream: The Path to a Better Future* (New York: Simon & Schuster, 2020), 131.

40 Pope Francis, "Letter of His Holiness Pope Francis to the Popular Movements," *Vatican.va*, April 12, 2020, https://www.vatican.va/content/francesco/en/letters/2020/documents/papa-francesco_20200412_lettera-movimentipopolari.html.
41 James P. Bailey, *Rethinking Poverty: Income, Assets, and the Catholic Social Justice Tradition* (Notre Dame, IN: University of Notre Dame Press, 2010), 50.
42 Bailey, *Rethinking Poverty*, 14–15.
43 Schneider and Harknett, "Work-Schedule Instability"; Molly Weston Williamson, "The State of Paid Family and Medical Leave in the U.S. in 2023," *Center for American Progress* (blog), January 5, 2023, https://www.americanprogress.org/article/the-state-of-paid-family-and-medical-leave-in-the-u-s-in-2023/.

7

Building Work We Can Live With

Chapter Outline

What Government Can Do	144
What Direct Employers Should Do	147
What Workers Can Do	148
Conclusion	154

So far, we've discussed Catholic social teaching's inclusive definition of work; what it means to think about work as paid or unpaid; how work can be good for us; the importance of leisure and rest; and what fair compensation for paid or unpaid work looks like. This final chapter will discuss concrete things workers can do ourselves, with colleagues, and through our political system to craft working conditions that help us lead meaningful lives. Catholic social teaching holds that work at its best can be a setting for "rich personal growth, where many aspects of life enter into play: creativity, planning for the future, developing our talents, living out our values, relating to others, giving glory to God" (*LS'* 127). Government is the representative of the whole community, acting on behalf of people whose relational nature has brought them together into society, and is powerful enough to protect workers against the whims of markets and employers. Direct employers have much they can do to respect workers' dignity and rights, and we should not accept the assumption that employers will exploit workers as far as they can; as humans, employers are capable of striving toward transcendence by making moral decisions. And workers ourselves have more power than we often think in working toward just conditions where we do work that is good for us. Forming unions, and working together in other collective ways, is an effective way for workers to defend their rights, strongly endorsed by Catholic social teaching.

What Government Can Do

Catholic social teaching has always seen it as legitimate, in fact important, for the government to defend workers' rights on behalf of the whole community. As Leo XIII wrote, "The mass of the poor have no resources of their own to fall back upon, and must chiefly depend upon the assistance of the State. And it is for this reason that wage-earners, since they mostly belong in the mass of the needy, should be specially cared for and protected by the government" (*RN* 37). This is a clear acknowledgment of the fact that one can be working and still be in poverty. It also commits the government to defending workers when market conditions leave them unable to survive. John Paul II explained that Leo was concerned about the idea that workers should be free to accept any wage, even an exploitatively low one. Opposing this, the Catholic tradition holds that the "public authority" must intervene to guarantee that workers can survive on their wages, because work is the only way they can exercise their human right to life (*CA* 8).

Catholic social teaching sees the government as having many responsibilities for protecting just working conditions and wages. The government does not work toward these goals either by taking over all economic activity or by allowing workers to fend for themselves. Rather, it pursues workers' rights both indirectly, "by creating favorable conditions for the free exercise of economic activity, which will lead to abundant opportunities for employment and sources of wealth," and directly, "by defending the weakest, by placing certain limits on the autonomy of the parties who determine working conditions, and by ensuring in every case the necessary minimum support for the unemployed worker" (*CA* 15). An example of creating favorable conditions for the exercise of economic activity might be doing away with regulations that place unnecessary burdens on small businesses. Many US states are easing regulatory burdens on work like home food preparation, food trucks, and hair braiding to create favorable conditions for people to start businesses and build wealth.[1] Laws mandating minimum wages, restricting child labor, and guaranteeing unemployment support through taxing employers are current US examples of direct government intervention in just wages and working conditions. Enforcing laws that govern workplace safety, protect workers' right to form unions, and punish hiring discrimination and workplace harassment is another way the government can protect workers against the greater economic power of their employers.

Catholic social teaching assigns responsibility according to the principle of subsidiarity, meaning that problems should be solved at the appropriate level of authority. Local communities and organizations should handle what they are able to, and higher levels of governmental authority should intervene only when a problem is serious enough or complex enough to require it (*QA* 79–80, *CA* 15, 48). Given the significant power imbalance between a worker who needs wages and their employer, Catholic social teaching sees the government as the appropriate authority to defend workers' interests. A "free economy" requires an equal playing field, so the government should intervene to stop monopolies and to defend workers' rights in their relationship with their employers (*CA* 48). Rights the government should work for include unemployment insurance; the guarantee of just wages through education, training, and laws; "humane working hours and adequate free time"; and protection from discrimination at work (*CA* 15).

The Catholic social teaching documents do not usually specify how government should ensure just wages or benefits. For example, the government could ensure just wages by providing family grants or universal basic income or by enforcing a minimum wage law. Retirement security could be provided as a national benefit or by passing a law requiring employers to provide it. In the United States today, some point out that government assistance such as Medicaid (health care assistance for low-income people) or the earned income tax credit (which lowers the amount of tax low-income workers owe, meaning they receive a check after filing their taxes) essentially subsidizes employers in paying unjustly low wages. A 2020 study by the Government Accountability Office found that "a sizable number of the recipients of federal aid programs such as Medicaid and food stamps are employed by some of the biggest and more profitable companies in the United States, chief among them Walmart and

McDonald's."[2] Catholic social teaching holds that an employer's obligation to provide just wages does not require the company to endanger its own financial sustainability. But when a company like Walmart makes billions in yearly profits while paying its workers so little that many qualify for public assistance, it is clearly evading its responsibility to pay just wages.[3]

A group of human resources executives in Catholic healthcare systems was probably thinking about situations like this when they wrote that "Catholic social teaching says it is wrong to encourage employees to opt into the welfare system instead of providing them with employer-sponsored benefits."[4] In this statement, the executives called on Catholic health care companies to provide health insurance to all their employees. Certainly, when large health care providers encourage needy employees to sign up for Medicaid instead of providing them health coverage, the hypocrisy is obvious. That said, Catholic social teaching does not require employers to provide all the benefits workers are entitled to on their own. The tradition envisions employers and the government working together to ensure workers receive just wages, health care, retirement security, and the other benefits that are their right. Many wealthier nations provide health care to all workers—waged and unpaid alike—through a universal health care system. This is not only fine, but even praiseworthy, from the perspective of Catholic social teaching, evidence of a community caring for its own members. It's true that in the United States, health care is commonly provided as an employer benefit, and it is particularly hypocritical for employers in the health care business to refuse this benefit to their own employees. The risk of employers taking advantage of government programs to underpay their workers is real. Still, Catholic social teaching does not prohibit direct employers and government as the indirect employer from collaborating to ensure workers a dignified life. Quite the contrary: providing benefits to the whole population may be one of the ways government can help create the conditions for businesses to thrive, by supporting workers' education and health and taking costs for health care and retirement off the plates of business owners.

This section focused on what government can do because of Catholic social teaching's desire for the government to take a strong role in protecting workers from harm by employers and by the free market, a vision where current practice in the United States often falls short. But government is not the only "indirect employer" whose actions shape the choices available to direct employers. Nonprofit groups and unions shape working conditions through their advocacy, lobbying of governments, and pressure tactics. For example, the Coalition of Immokalee Workers, discussed in Chapter 4, won wage and safety improvements for farmworkers by pressuring food buyers, rather than farm owners, to agree to higher costs and a labor code of conduct.[5] Local and statewide minimum wage laws are often supported by religious organizations, as are initiatives to provide family grants, child care subsidies, health care, and other benefits to working families. And pressure campaigns from customers, using social media or the power of the boycott, can encourage direct employers to improve wages or conditions or to recognize a workers' union.

What Direct Employers Should Do

Even outside Catholic social teaching, most people intuitively see the direct employer as the one most responsible for workers' just treatment and well-being, which explains why gig-economy businesses like Uber go to such lengths to argue that the workers who make a living from their apps are not their employees. For Catholic social teaching, direct employers are responsible for offering just wages and working conditions because the employer controls the property workers use in their work. This privileged position bears the responsibility for using property justly. Owners of any property—even the money to pay wages—have a responsibility to direct it to its true purpose: serving good, dignified human work. "Ownership morally justifies itself in the creation, at the proper time and in the proper way, of opportunities for work and human growth for all," John Paul II wrote. Investing capital should "offer people an opportunity to make good use of their own labor" (*CA* 43, 36). "Business management cannot concern itself only with the interests of the proprietors," Benedict XVI added, "but must also assume responsibility for all the other stakeholders who contribute to the life of the business: the workers, the clients, the suppliers of various elements of production, the community" (*CV* 40). A recent document published by two Vatican teaching offices strongly insists: "No profit is in fact legitimate when it falls short of the objective of the integral promotion of the human person, the universal destination of goods, and the preferential option for the poor" (*Oeconomicae et Pecuniariae Quaestiones* 10).

Catholic social teaching's expectation that employers would pay just wages because they understand it as their duty, without being forced to do so by laws, worker organizing, or consumer pressure, is not as idealistic as it may sound. As of this writing, nearly 400 global companies have signed onto the United Nations' Forward Faster compact, committing to the goal of paying 100 percent of employees a living wage by 2030.[6] France's Michelin tire company committed to "a salary enabling a family of four to live 'decently' in the city where they work . . . paying basic expenses and being able to save and spend modestly on goods or leisure activities."[7] Michelin's chief executive, Florent Menegaux, believed that decent pay improves worker engagement and performance, and said that "when a salary doesn't pay enough for one person to project himself or herself into the future, it's a problem."[8] These insights echo Leo XIII's understanding that a just wage allows a worker to plan for the future. Other business leaders note that living wages reduce employee turnover, improve the company's image, and reduce conflict between managers and workers.[9] Catholic social teaching would applaud these businesses for finding a way to align their interests in the market with their employees' human dignity. In light of that, I am always surprised that US businesses rarely advocate for universal health care and other safety nets, which would provide more security to workers while saving themselves significant costs as employers. For a community and employers to share the responsibility of providing workers a just wage and benefits is part of the vision of Catholic social teaching.

What Workers Can Do

Many books on work talk about what workers can do to improve pay and working conditions in terms of individual decision-making. Readers of this book will have to go elsewhere for tips on developing your skills or networking to move into a job with better working conditions. The individualistic advice that workers can improve conditions by leaving certain jobs presumes that certain jobs will always be underpaid, dangerous, or disrespected, which is not something Catholic social teaching accepts. Rather, no matter the job tasks or title, workers have a right to family-supporting wages and safe, dignified conditions. We fulfill our relational human nature by fighting for these rights together.

The Catholic tradition knows that workers' agency is behind everything useful that work produces. Work is a human activity, which means it is creative and social. Many factors contribute to unjust wages and working conditions, including unequal global trade, political shifts in the desire to keep workers safe, and lobbying from businesses that want cheap labor above all. That said, workers provide the good that employers want: their labor. This gives workers immense power in the struggle for more just pay and conditions. And this power is greatly amplified when workers join together.

Chapter 2 mentioned how Catholic social teaching strongly supports workers forming labor unions. This is not just because unions tend to win better wages and benefits for their members, bringing jobs more in line with the Church's understanding of worker justice. It is because to join with others is part of our relational nature as human beings, and to deny someone that right—even at work—is to deny their humanity. Opposing human rights, including "the freedom to organize and to form unions," "impoverish[es] the human person as much as, if not more than, the deprivation of material goods" (*SRS* 15). Taking action through unions is good for workers. Like any relationship where we trust each other and work together for a common goal, union activity helps people express their creative and social nature, to "realize their humanity more fully in every respect" (*LE* 15, 20).

Many people assume that workers unionize in order to secure better pay and benefits, and this is indeed a common result. In studies comparing similar jobs and workplaces, workers in unions enjoy wages that are 10 to 15 percent higher than nonunionized workers.[10] Unionized workers are more likely to have employer-provided benefits for health care and retirement, and even less common benefits such as child care and commuting support, than nonunionized workers.[11] The union difference adds up over time, as workers in unions are more likely to own homes and have on average more than $100,000 more in savings than non-unionized workers.[12] Union contracts typically include language protecting workers in the event of layoffs or firing, in contrast with the "at-will" employment typical in nonunionized workplaces, where workers can lose their jobs at any time for any reason. During the Covid-19 pandemic, unionized workers used their power to negotiate furloughs or work-share agreements instead of layoffs, one reason that industries with higher union representation saw fewer job losses during that time of serious upheaval.[13]

In addition to these better-known benefits, unionization offers a voice for workers to address needs specific to their profession. For example, unions of health care providers negotiate for safe staffing levels and adequate personal protective equipment. Teachers' unions advocate for class sizes that are best for effective education. United Farm Workers (UFW) victories include regulations on work in extreme heat, a successful pressure campaign against a dangerous pesticide, and a ban on a particular farm tool that caused debilitating pain and back injuries.[14] Since UFW pursues these goals at the statewide or industry-wide level, their victories also protect workers who are not UFW members. The Writers Guild of America (WGA) and the actors' union SAG-AFTRA won contract commitments preventing film and TV studios from using generative AI to replace writers and performers (thanks to the strike discussed below).[15] One reason Starbucks workers have formed unions around the country in recent years is to combat unpredictable scheduling, which interferes with adequate rest and a normal routine for many retail and service workers.[16] And a union for adult film performers provides a "consent checklist" to help workers protect their personal boundaries on set.[17] Workers need different things in order to be safe, healthy, and to do their work well, and they are in the best position to know what they need for their particular job. Workers in a union have a reliable way to have their voice heard at work for the compensation and protections they need, and a powerful voice to pressure government to do its job protecting workers.

Catholic social teaching specifically defends workers' right to strike, withholding their labor to pressure employers to agree to fairer wages or conditions. Striking workers agree to forgo their work and their wages, strategizing that their employer will not be able to replace their labor quickly and will agree to their demands in order to get them back to work. This right, like all other rights of workers, stems from human nature. Because humans are free and responsible, they have a right to choose when and why to work or to withhold their labor. Strikes should inspire the "public authority" to intervene in the matter of unjust wages, hours, conditions, or whatever pushed the workers to action (*RN* 39). The right to strike should be protected, while workers should realize that it is an "extreme" action that should not be abused (*LE* 20).

Recent high-profile strikes in the United States have demonstrated the power workers have to effect change when they withhold their labor. A few examples are the Writers Guild of America (WGA) strike in 2023, which halted the production of new films and TV for 148 days, also affecting celebrity media appearances as members of performers' unions refused to promote new work in solidarity with the writers. With every TV watcher in the United States affected by the work stoppage, writers won a fairer percentage of pay from streaming media and protections from AI competition.[18] A strike of port workers in 2024 threatened to upset supply chains across the United States, but workers called it off after only two days when employers agreed to a 62 percent wage increase.[19] Part of the reality of work's social nature is that our work never only affects ourselves; it contributes to the world in ways people may take for granted. Joining with coworkers to stop work makes it clear how much our community depends on our labor. A strike is an effective, although last-resort, way to win significant improvements in wages and workplace conditions.

Union activity—attending meetings, hashing out bargaining agreements, speaking with colleagues about their concerns and priorities—is clearly work in the understanding of Catholic social teaching, even though it involves different tasks than may be part of our paid job.[20] Workers who are involved in forming a union or taking action through a union on their coworkers' behalf spend numerous hours outside their paid job involved in the work of organizing. Gaining and keeping the protection of a union at your workplace is not easy, but it can be profoundly rewarding and effective work. Katherine Wilson, an adjunct faculty member who helped successfully organize and lead a union for her colleagues at Fordham, commented, "There is no question that the only time I have felt dignified working in a university was the activist work in the union here. That is the most dignified relationship I have had."[21] Workers in unions reap the benefits of the voluntary work of many people, leading to benefits in pay and security no one of them could achieve on their own.

When people show up and sacrifice for others because they understand their interests are linked, we call that solidarity. Catholic social teaching talks about solidarity as both a reality and a moral commitment. It is a reality because the interests of all people are linked with one another, even if those people's lives appear to be very different, and whether they realize it or not. Solidarity is a moral commitment or a virtue (a moral quality of a person) when people realize that our interests are linked and try their best to live in light of that reality. Theologian Bryan Massingale says that solidarity "leads us to recognize our responsibility for one another and how we are really given to each other's care."²² John Paul II calls it "a firm and persevering determination to commit oneself to the common good; that is to say to the good of all and of each individual, because we are all really responsible for all" (*SRS* 38). An example of solidarity is "the fact that men and women in various parts of the world feel personally affected by the injustices and violations of human rights committed in distant countries, countries which perhaps they will never visit" (*SRS* 37). And Pope Francis quite simply calls solidarity "a way of making history" (*FT* 116).

Besides Catholic social teaching, one place you often hear the word "solidarity" used is in labor union contexts. When one group of unionized workers supports another's boycott or contributes to their strike fund, they proudly talk about doing so in solidarity, recognizing that all workers' interests are united. "Solidarity is a process of love, blended with power and directed," labor journalist Sarah Jaffe writes. "Solidarity doesn't mean you have to like every person you're fighting alongside. But in those moments when you stand shoulder to shoulder, you do love one another."²³

One of my favorite examples of solidarity in action comes from the state of Indiana, where a university doing a major construction project hired a mix of building trades union members, who were mostly US citizens, and undocumented workers who were not union members. The scene was set for the unionized workers to turn against the more vulnerable, undocumented builders, but instead, they invited them to union meetings and joined with them to defend job site safety and fair pay. Rather than treating the undocumented workers as possible competition undercutting what they had, the union workers saw that they would all be better off if they could get the undocumented workers the same protections they themselves enjoyed. For their part, the undocumented workers displayed solidarity by trusting the union workers enough to take action together with them, despite their own precarious status.²⁴

This story also gives us my favorite alternative definition of solidarity. Labor leader Tom Lewandowski described the union position toward the undocumented workers as "If they're getting [screwed], we're getting [screwed]."²⁵ Catholic social teaching clearly distinguishes solidarity from charity or compassion. Solidarity is not about helping someone else because you pity them, or feel sad that they are suffering (*SRS* 38, *FT* 116).

It is about realizing that in a real way, we all benefit when others have safe workplaces, family-supporting wages, and health care. And when our neighbors, friends, and family members risk injury at work, can't support themselves on their wages, or can't see a doctor when they're sick, we all lose. If they're getting screwed, we're getting screwed! Or the flip side: when we have solidarity, we are willing to work hard on behalf of others because we recognize that we are all connected. If we can help someone who's currently struggling get to a position to take care of themselves and one day help others, our whole community will be better off.

Alison Green, who writes the popular work advice blog Ask a Manager, frequently advises readers with workplace problems to "push back as a group," calmly raising concerns as a group of colleagues together, in person.[26] Collective pushback by a group can be more effective than one person speaking up about an issue that affects many employees, like a cut to benefits. Support from colleagues is also crucial when employers are hiding unjust practices, like paying women less than men for the same work. Although it takes place outside the legal framework of union organizing, such collective workplace action is another form of solidarity. Each worker must trust the others enough to take the risk of speaking up about an unpopular or unjust policy, recognizing that any risk is less because it is shared among many, and any success will be greater because it benefits everyone.

Finally, we have some power in managing what is wrong with the unpaid work and the balance of work and leisure in our lives. I hope it helps to know that our unpaid work is important, that it connects us with others, and that it can be a source of joy, meaning, and creativity that helps us complete the stress cycle. Empowered with that knowledge, we can ask different questions about our unpaid work. Is this work alienating because it doesn't allow us adequate time for rest and social connection? Maybe a partner or other family member needs to "lean in" to their share of caregiving or housework. Is unpaid work restorative in some instances and draining in others? For example, I find cooking restorative when I have enough time to experience flow in the task, but I am happy to outsource the daily provision of lunch to my kid's public school. And when I advocate for policies like family leave and universal basic income that could help support others in doing the unpaid work that is so crucial to my community's well-being, I feel proud knowing I might be helping the working conditions of other unpaid workers in the future.

How about rest and leisure? Are we spending too much time on tasks that generate acedia, like TV or social media, and not enough on the unpaid work that can restore our bodies and spirits? Maybe there's an opportunity to take up a new hobby or create a new habit. Similarly, can we build time into our lives to experience leisure, intentional "doing nothing" whose purpose is not to rest for work? A weekly practice of time outdoors, a social media Sabbath, dinner with friends, or showing up for prayer or worship can bring us back to the human creatures we are, prior to and beyond our productivity as workers. The solutions here will vary as much as workers, and their unique responsibilities, do. And—like solutions to problems with our paid work—many will call for solidarity from others, requiring us to lean into the vulnerability of our nature to ask for help. The message of Catholic social teaching is consistent: when work is bad, it doesn't have to be this way; work can be good for us. This is true whether we are talking about paid or unpaid work, whenever work is interfering with our human right to the leisure that restores us to be who we truly are.

Conclusion

This book's final chapter highlighted concrete ways governments, direct employers, and workers themselves can move toward Catholic social teaching's vision of justice for work, whether paid or unpaid. Governments have an important role in defending workers' rights against the greater power of employers and can even provide some of the benefits, such as health care or retirement security, that are the right of every worker. Direct employers should offer safe conditions and just wages, and increasingly, some recognize that worker-friendly conditions are also good for business. Workers themselves have significant power to win better pay and conditions when they join together, whether through legally recognized unions or less formal communities of solidarity. Finally, understanding how work, rest, and leisure are all important and necessary can help us as individuals to reflect on the balance of these three goods in our own lives and draw on our families and communities for help making any necessary changes.

Work is important: it develops our abilities, connects us with others, and most often, is the way we provide for ourselves and our families. Work is important enough in our lives that we should expect that it can be better than it is, and work toward that reality. Many people today are rejecting the religion of "workism" that says we must be defined by our constant productivity, but they may not know where to look for new ideas about work. Catholic social teaching's message to workers overwhelmed by the state of work today is this: there's nothing wrong with you for wanting a job that supports you and leaves time for the rest of life; you have a right to a life (and a work life) of meaning and purpose; and you have more power than you might think to make it happen. Thinking seriously about what work is, its place in a meaningful life, and how communities can fairly compensate the work that keeps them running is the first step to getting there, for every one of us. Whether you are Catholic or not, Catholic social teaching's inclusive definition of work is a good place to start.

When we come to understand that work is not just what we do for pay, but any activity where we use our abilities to shape the things around us and ourselves, a new way of prioritizing our days, weeks, and years opens up to us. Our calling, our vocation, is more than a paid job, so we understand that we still have dignity and worth if we are not currently working for pay, or if our paid work is not high in status. Since our paid work is not our life's primary source of meaning, we might be less afraid to challenge a job's status quo, whether that means placing better boundaries around our working hours, refusing work that causes alienation or moral injury, or standing in solidarity with coworkers to win better wages and working conditions for all of us. When we recognize that work is more important for how it changes the worker than for what it produces, we see how important it is to find work that forms us for the good and resist work that harms us in body, mind, or spirit.

Catholic social teaching's inclusive definition of work can change our perspective on unpaid work, too. We can see unpaid work, including volunteering, art, and family caregiving, as the skilled, creative, crucial contribution to the community that it is. We can recognize that a policy like universal basic income is not a handout, but fair compensation for all the value unpaid work contributes to building up our communities and making paid work possible. When we think about our own unpaid work, we can manage our own expectations and be gentle with ourselves when hours of home chores after a full paid workday become overwhelming—it's all work, after all. We can recognize, too, that unpaid work can be good for us, helping us complete the stress cycle and care for our embodied selves. Perhaps seeking out this benefit in our unpaid work will help us find a better balance, not alone, but with the help of family and community. And since we know that we are body, mind, and spirit, we are not surprised that we need leisure as well as work, as good as work can be for us. We can resist the cultural pressure to be always active and changing things, instead building in intentional time in worship, in nature, and with loved ones to receive the gifts of our life and celebrate them, just as they are.

When we recognize that work is something everyone does, and that every person has innate dignity regardless of the status or pay of the work they do, we reject with particular venom the idea that some jobs will always be dangerous or pay too little to live on, and that workers enduring such conditions must deserve it. We can see that workers in climate-controlled offices have more in common than not with workers picking fruit, catching fish, driving trucks, or emptying bedpans. If they're getting screwed, we're getting screwed, and the solution is solidarity, to know and act on the fact that we are all responsible for one another. We can recognize that indirect employers such as government determine the laws, regulations, and trade agreements that shape wages and working conditions, and we can make clear that we expect our governments to build economies where each person can access basic needs, rest, and leisure, whether or not they currently work for pay.

When we pay attention to the many things that are wrong with work today, it can feel difficult to imagine that the world could ever change. But Catholic social teaching's inclusive definition of work reminds us that the world changes when humans apply our creative and relational abilities to the people and things around us, including ourselves. We change the world when we plant, produce, transport, build, clean, create, or sell. We change others when we care, heal, communicate, teach, listen, organize, and lead. We change ourselves as we move, learn, practice, reflect, or open our minds to something new. Our life's meaning, our human dignity, does not depend on work, but still, our work, paid or unpaid, changes the world. Understanding this is a gift. May each of us receive it, celebrate it, and use it well in our unique vocation of making a life.

Notes

1 Karen Hawkins, "Hair-Braiding Bill Offers Regulatory Compromise," *The State Journal-Register*, May 2, 2010, https://www.sj-r.com/story/

news/2010/05/02/hair-braiding-bill-offers-regulatory/44222113007/; Laura Ferguson, "Food Trucks as a Force for Social Justice," *Tufts Now*, April 19, 2018, https://now.tufts.edu/2018/04/19/food-trucks-force-social-justice.

2   Eli Rosenberg, "Walmart and McDonald's Have the Most Workers on Food Stamps and Medicaid, New Study Shows," *Washington Post*, November 18, 2020, https://www.washingtonpost.com/business/2020/11/18/food-stamps-medicaid-mcdonalds-walmart-bernie-sanders/.

3   Annett, *Cathonomics*, 156.

4   Jeffrey W. Hamlin, "A 'Just Wage': More Than Dollars," *Health Progress: Journal of the Catholic Health Association of the United States*, April 2002, https://www.chausa.org/publications/health-progress/archive/article/march-april-2002/a-just-wage-more-than-dollars.

5   Holly Burkhalter, "Fair Food Program Helps End the Use of Slavery in the Tomato Fields," *Washington Post*, September 2, 2012, https://www.washingtonpost.com/opinions/fair-food-program-helps-end-the-use-of-slavery-in-the-tomato-fields/2012/09/02/788f1a1a-f39c-11e1-892d-bc92fee603a7_story.html.

6   "Companies Taking Action | Forward Faster," https://forwardfaster.unglobalcompact.org/companies-taking-action (accessed May 3, 2024).

7   Liz Alderman, "What Is a 'Decent Wage'? France's Michelin Raises a Debate," *The New York Times*, April 26, 2024, https://www.nytimes.com/2024/04/26/business/france-michelin-wages.html.

8   Alderman, "What Is a 'Decent Wage'?"

9   Sanda Ojiambo, "Why Companies Must Pay Living Wages to Fully Benefit Society," *World Economic Forum*, May 14, 2024, https://www.weforum.org/stories/2024/05/why-companies-must-pay-living-wages/.

10 Laura Feiveson, "Labor Unions and the U.S. Economy," U.S. Department of the Treasury, August 28, 2023, https://home.treasury.gov/news/featured-stories/labor-unions-and-the-us-economy.

11 Feiveson, "Labor Unions and the U.S. Economy."

12 Emily Peck, "There's a Wealth Gap between Union and Nonunion Workers," *Axios*, March 20, 2024, https://www.axios.com/2024/03/20/union-workers-wealth-comparison-pay-difference.

13 Celine McNicholas, Heidi Shierholz, and Margaret Poydock, "Union Workers Had More Job Security during the Pandemic, but Unionization Remains Historically Low," *Economic Policy Institute*, January 22, 2021, https://www.epi.org/publication/union-workers-had-more-job-security-during-the-pandemic-but-unionization-remains-historically-low-data-on-union-representation-in-2020-reinforce-the-need-for-dismantling-barriers-to-union-organizing/.

14. Jocelyn Sherman, "National Heat Regs," *United Farm Workers*, January 28, 2023, https://ufw.org/national-heat-regs/; admin, "Methyl Iodide," *United Farm Workers* (blog), February 19, 2017, https://ufw.org/methyl-iodide/; n.a., "El Cortito," *National Farm Worker Ministry's 50 for 50* (blog), https://nfwm.org/50for50/artwork/el-cortito/ (accessed December 5, 2024).
15. Cant, Muldoon, and Graham, *Feeding the Machine*, 97.
16. n.a., "Our Fight," *Starbucks Workers United*, https://sbworkersunited.org/our-fight/ (accessed December 5, 2024).
17. Amelia Pollard, "Hot Union Summer Comes to the Porn Industry," *The American Prospect*, August 23, 2021, https://prospect.org/api/content/8e75414e-0204-11ec-acdd-1244d5f7c7c6/.
18. Annabelle Timsit, "Hollywood Studios and Writers Have a Strike-Ending Deal. What's in It?," *Washington Post*, September 27, 2023, https://www.washingtonpost.com/style/2023/09/27/wga-contract-details-writers-strike-deal/.
19. Ian Duncan et al., "Dockworkers Union Suspends Strike; Ports Reopen on East and Gulf Coasts," *Washington Post*, October 3, 2024, https://www.washingtonpost.com/business/2024/10/03/port-strike-over/.
20. Jaffe, *Work Won't Love You Back*, 259.
21. Jaffe, *Work Won't Love You Back*, 261–2.
22. Bryan N. Massingale, *Racial Justice and the Catholic Church* (Maryknoll, NY: Orbis Books, 2010), 116.
23. Jaffe, *Work Won't Love You Back*, 335.
24. Sarah Jaffe, "In GOP Country, a Small Labor Organization Offers a Model for Fighting Trumpism," *The Nation*, November 4, 2016, https://www.thenation.com/article/archive/in-gop-country-a-small-labor-organization-offers-a-model-for-fighting-trumpism/.
25. Jaffe. This is how I quote Mr. Lewandowski when I teach this story in class. Guess what he actually said?
26. Alison Green, "How to Speak up as a Group at Work," *Ask a Manager*, February 19, 2018, https://www.askamanager.org/2018/02/how-to-speak-up-as-a-group-at-work.html; Alison Green, "The Horrified New Hires, the Gift Exchange Revolt, and Other Times You Pushed Back as a Group at Work," *Ask a Manager*, September 19, 2024, https://www.askamanager.org/2024/09/the-horrified-new-hires-the-gift-exchange-revolt-and-other-times-you-pushed-back-as-a-group-at-work.html.

Discussion Questions

Chapter 1

This chapter discusses "workism," the idea that paid work is the most important thing in our lives and the source of our meaning and purpose. Do you agree that this idea is widespread in our culture, or in your community? Do you think it is a true idea, or one in need of challenging? How might humans find meaning and purpose if not through paid work?

For you personally, is the Catholic Church a trusted authority on questions like the purpose of human life, the nature of work, and economic justice? Why or why not? When you think about your current views on these questions, what authorities or sources have shaped your own views?

Is it important for someone's paid job to be connected to their vocation or calling in life? If you are currently working for pay, do you think of your job as your vocation, or part of your vocation? If someone's paid job is not their vocation, what are some examples of things that might be? Can you see any drawbacks to someone thinking of their paid job as a vocation or calling?

Do you believe that a human being is made up of body, mind, and spirit? Do you think our contemporary work culture takes into account all these parts of the human experience? Have the jobs you have worked in the past respected you as a person who is body, mind, and spirit?

Do you believe humans are interdependent—not ultimately independent, but made up of the relationships we have with others? Do you think our contemporary work culture treats workers as if they are interdependent? Have the jobs you have worked in the past respected you as a person who is interdependent with others?

Chapter 2

What do you think of Catholic social teaching's inclusive definition of work, in which work is any activity in which humans transform the world around us, whether done for pay or not? Is it odd to think of chores, caregiving, volunteering, and other unpaid activities as "work," or does that make sense to you? If more people in your community adopted this inclusive definition, what else might change?

"The priority of the subjective dimension of work" is Catholic social teaching's jargony way of saying that the impact of work on the worker is more important than whatever results the work produces. Do you agree with this? How might our laws, work policies, and educational systems look different if our communities accepted that the impact of work on the worker is more important than the results produced?

This chapter discusses education as one example of work that our culture values more for its subjective element (how it shapes workers) than its objective results (what is produced). Do you think this is true? Can you think of other examples of work that our culture values for how it shapes workers, rather than objective results?

Do you believe that all people who are able to work for pay have a duty to do so? Catholic social teaching says that all people who are able to work have a duty to do so, but that paid or unpaid work fulfills this duty. What do you think of that idea? What would change in our society if unpaid work, such as volunteering or family care, was widely viewed as fulfilling a duty to work in the same way as paid work does?

How does the work you are doing now—whether paid or unpaid—shape you as a person? Does it help you grow and flourish as a person, or is it harmful to your body, mind, or spirit? If so, is it harmful because of something intrinsic to the work, or because of something about your working conditions that could be changed?

Do you agree that it's possible for work to alienate us, harming us by distancing us from our own human nature? Have you ever done work that was alienating, or do you know anyone who does?

Some people believe that since work is supposed to be good for humans, work that is exploitative or alienating should not be considered work. Catholic social teaching disagrees: even bad or alienating work is still work. What is at stake in this disagreement? Who benefits when bad work (such as prison labor) is not considered work, and who benefits when work must be seen as good in order to qualify as work?

Chapter 3

Catholic social teaching sees unpaid care within the family as work. Does this make sense to you? If not, what do you see as the important distinctions between unpaid family care and work?

In your opinion, would family care receive more respect in society if more people thought of it as work? Would it receive more respect if it were compensated, for example, by government financial support to caregivers?

Are some people "naturally" good at care work, or can anyone develop the skills to be an effective caregiver? What are the reasons for your position?

Have you ever worked a job that required emotional labor, maintaining a particular emotion in yourself or others? Did you find it changed your experience of your emotions outside of the workday?

Have you ever given care as part of a paid job or your unpaid work? How do you think doing this work changed you as a person?

Some attempt to put a dollar value on unpaid care work, estimating the value of a stay-at-home mom's labor or the contributions of unpaid care work to the global economy. Do you think this is a helpful way to argue for the value and importance of care work, or is something lost when describing this work in economic terms?

Chapter 4

What were you doing the last time you experienced "flow" (p. 66)? Were you doing something that would be considered work in Catholic social teaching?

Have you ever engaged in an activity that Catholic social teaching would consider work as a way to help you deal with stress? Does it seem that physical or creative activities "complete the stress cycle" more effectively than passive activities such as watching videos?

Rebecca May Johnson and Matthew Crawford suggest that manual labor in which we deal with physical materials challenges our attention and skills in uniquely positive ways that can induce flow and other positive benefits of work. Has this been your experience of manual labor? Does the way these authors describe manual labor as skilled and attentive challenge or confirm your impression of this type of work?

I suggest that Catholic social teaching sees many types of work, not just manual labor, as an opportunity to challenge ourselves by encountering reality. Does any of the work you do (paid or unpaid) challenge you in a positive way by requiring you to meet external standards?

What do you know about the experiences of farmworkers in your community and the particular challenges they face? If you consume food produced in other countries, what do you know about the conditions for workers there?

Do you agree with the Catholic tradition's "universal destination of goods" that everyone has a right to meet their needs, but no one has a right to more than they need while others have less than they need? Why do you agree or disagree?

Catholic social teaching calls for expropriation in the unique case of *latifundia*. Due to land's unique purpose in providing food for human needs, "insufficiently cultivated estates should be distributed to those who can make these lands fruitful" (*GS* 71). Do you agree that government should redistribute farmland when it is not being used to produce food? Why or why not?

CST's call for redistribution of *latifundia* sees farmland as a unique type of property. Because its purpose is to meet human needs for food, farmable land is used against its own nature when it is treated as simply an investment. Are there other types of property that are so important to human needs that communities should set special ethical guidelines around their use? For example, is it unjust to keep housing empty, as an investment, when there are people in need of homes, or to price lifesaving drugs so high that some patients cannot afford them? Could you argue for your position based on ideas found in Catholic social teaching?

When you make choices about which food businesses to support or how much to tip a server, do you see yourself as an "indirect employer" of food workers? Do you think the choices of individual consumers can lead to better pay and safer conditions for food workers, or is it better to focus on passing laws to protect these workers, viewing the government as the "indirect employer?"

What do you think of the proposal to see food, and even manufactured items, as sacramental, making present for us the reality of the human work that brought us these things that we need? Do you already think of the goods you consume in terms of the work it took to produce them? Do you agree that practices such as avoiding food waste, or passing things we no longer need along to others who can use them, are respectful of the work that went into producing these goods?

Chapter 5

How does the experience of leisure—the receptive state of accepting the world as it is and celebrating its goodness—feel to you? Is this a common experience for you, or is it rare? The last time you experienced leisure, who were you with and what were you doing?

Psychologist Mihaly Csikszentmihalyi believes we would be better off if we used our free time in active pursuits where we might experience flow, rather than in passive activities such as watching TV. Do you agree? Which active free-time practices do you find personally restorative? After doing passive activities such as watching TV or scrolling social media, how do you feel?

Tricia Hersey and Jenny Odell argue that intentional nonactivity—rest or "doing nothing"—is good for us in ways that go far beyond preparing us to do more work. Restoring our imagination and attention and resisting workism or "hustle culture" are some of the benefits they see in intentional nonactivity. Do you agree? How often do you experience intentional nonactivity?

Do you think of artmaking as work, play, or something else? What are the key elements of artmaking that help you see it this way?

Many of the artists quoted in this chapter spoke about a deep inner compulsion to make their art, in terms including vocation, "I'm meant to do it," "I can't help it," and "Nothing can stop me." Do you feel this strong intrinsic motivation about any of your own work activities, paid or unpaid? How does this affect how you prioritize this work in your life?

If paid work is part of your life, does the extrinsic motivation of earning money affect your enjoyment of it, how you approach the work, and how you balance paid and unpaid work in your life? Are there aspects of your paid work that you would still do if you were not paid?

Artmaking can be viewed as therapeutic, helping artists "figure things out," imagine the future, and cope with challenges or profound loss. Does any of the (paid or unpaid) work you engage in help you in these ways?

Does your community currently have any "structures for inoperativity," in the words of theologian Andrew Blosser, such as laws limiting the hours or days people can work, customs of closing stores and other public places on particular days, or universal basic income to help people survive if they are not currently working for pay? Do you think people and communities would benefit from "structures of inoperativity"?

Chapter 6

Do you agree with Catholic social teaching that economic coercion can occur, that workers can be forced by financial necessity to accept pay or working conditions they would not otherwise agree to? Do you think economic coercion is common or rare? What systems would a community need to put in place to make sure that workers are truly free to choose jobs with pay and conditions that are fair to them?

Does the concept of the indirect employer—large-scale entities that set the economic conditions affecting direct employers, such as laws and trade agreements—make sense to you? What do you know about the factors affecting working conditions and wages for workers in your community? Which indirect employers might be in a position to make things better?

Do you think "disgraceful working conditions, where [workers] are treated as mere tools for profit, rather than as free and responsible persons" (*GS* 27) are common or rare in your community and throughout the world? Do you agree with Catholic social teaching that working conditions treating people as tools for profit are a serious violation of human dignity? Why or why not?

What do you know about the situation of migrants in your community? What types of jobs do they typically do, and what are the pay and working conditions like? What do you know about the reasons migrants to your community leave their original homes? How is your community doing at moving toward the goal to "welcome, protect, promote and integrate (*FT* 129)" migrants?

Try to figure out what income is necessary for a single person, a single parent, or a family of four to meet their basic needs in your community. (If you are in the United States, you can use United Way's ALICE Budget and Income Status Tool at unitedforalice.org/alice-income-status-tool, or look up American Compass's Cost-of-Thriving Index (COTI), which estimates major costs for a family of four.) Then, look at employment listings to get a sense of the jobs that are available in your community and figure out whether the wages they offer can support a family's basic needs. Can a retail worker in your community support their basic needs as a single person? Can a teacher support a family?

What programs are available in your community to support people who are working and still unable to afford their basic needs? Who provides funding for those programs? What do you think would have to change for employers in your community to pay workers enough to meet their basic needs without other support?

Evaluate CST's concrete policies aimed at worker justice, including family wage, family grants, and universal basic income. How does each policy succeed or fail at ensuring worker dignity, support for families, gender equality, and support for unpaid caregiving work? Which policy might work best in your community? How would your own life, or plans for your life, change if your community had such a policy in place?

Chapter 7

What are some things the government where you are is doing to protect workers' rights? What are some things they could be doing differently?

Do you think it is better for governments to require employers to provide workers with just wages and benefits, or for the government to provide certain benefits (such as healthcare) to everyone? What are the pros and cons of each approach for workers, employers, and members of the community not currently working for pay?

Find out what it is like to form a union for workers in your community. Which industries or professions commonly have workplace unions and which do not? Are any professions forbidden by law from unionizing? Choose a profession you are interested in, or one you interact with on a regular basis, and research the types of issues workers in that profession might want to resolve in a union contract, or the typical wage differential for unionized vs. nonunionized workers.

When have you experienced solidarity from someone you work with, or shown solidarity to someone at work or in your community? What results came about from realizing that your interests were aligned and acting on that fact?

Think about the paid and unpaid work you do and the balance of work, rest, and leisure in your life. What is in your power to change, and what would need support from others in order to change? How might you advocate for yourself, ask for help, and make wise decisions about your own use of time to achieve justice in your paid and unpaid work and adequate time for rest and leisure?

Glossary

Please consult the Index for more information on each of these terms and the people mentioned in the definitions.

Acedia: an unhappy state of mind where we are unable to settle down to either work or relaxation, instead occupying ourselves with distractions. Traditionally understood as **sin** because it indicates a failure to accept our own human nature, which benefits from both work and rest.

ALICE: an acronym created by the nonprofit United Way to draw attention to the high percentage of US people who cannot afford to meet basic needs despite working for pay. It stands for Asset Limited, Income Constrained, Employed.

Alienating work: in **Catholic social teaching**, work is alienating when it separates the worker from their human nature. This can happen when work exploits human bodies or misuses the human abilities for creativity and connection, or when it gives workers no chance to exercise those abilities.

Basic income see Universal basic income

Burnout: the inability to work due to exhaustion, a sense that work is pointless, or both; can result from economic or internal pressure to work beyond our capacity for a long time.

Catholic social teaching: the tradition of commentary on economic, social, and political life from Catholic popes and bishops since 1891. All Catholics are expected to make a good-faith effort to know and follow Catholic social teaching.

Common good: the good for a whole community and for all members of the community, especially the most vulnerable. **Catholic social teaching** says that individual persons, leaders of a community, and businesses must all pursue the common good as their goal.

Constitution (papal teaching document): Church Councils publish these teaching documents which hold even higher authority than papal **encyclicals**, because they reflect the consultation of all the bishops of the global Catholic Church.

Creation: Everything God has made for humans, including things found in nature, things humans make out of things found in nature, and humans themselves—basically, everything that exists in the world.

CST: an abbreviation for **Catholic social teaching**.

Direct employer: the person or company we would traditionally think of as an employer, who determines a worker's pay and working conditions directly, in contrast to the **indirect employer**.

Economic coercion: when people feel forced to do things, such as accept a job with subpar wages or dangerous working conditions, because they have no better option for economic survival.

Embodiment: The Catholic understanding that human persons are body-spirit beings. Both bodily and spiritual existence are important to human life and cannot be dismissed. See **incarnational.**

Emotional labor: managing our own or others' feelings, or displaying a certain emotion, as part of the requirements of a paid job, coined by the sociologist Arlie Hochschild.

Encyclical: a document published by a pope when he intends to signal that he is teaching authoritatively as part of the Church's tradition. **Catholic social teaching** has primarily been taught through papal encyclicals.

Expropriation: when the government takes private property or changes the laws that allow property to be privately owned.

Family grants: John Paul II was the first pope to propose that government should make cash payments to families as a way of supporting the unpaid labor of caring for children.

Family wage: a wage on which one full-time worker can support a family, the oldest proposal for a **just wage** in **Catholic social teaching**.

Flow: a pleasant feeling of deep immersion and time passing quickly that occurs when we are engaged in a task where the challenge level meets our skills, as named by the psychologist Mihaly Csikszentmihalyi.

Grind culture: the idea that people can thrive under capitalism by constantly working and optimizing their productivity, as described by theologian Tricia Hersey. See also **total work, workism.**

Incarnational: Incarnation is the Christian belief that God took on human flesh in the person of Jesus. Human reality is therefore incarnational, defined by both bodily and spiritual existence. See **embodiment**.

Inclusive definition of work: Work in **Catholic social teaching** is any activity where humans use our abilities to transform **creation**, whether or not we are paid for that activity and whether it is good for us or exploitative.

Indirect employer: persons or groups who affect workers' pay and conditions indirectly by shaping markets and public policy, such as governments.

Inoperativity: "intentional actions or states of being that have no purposive quality outside themselves," according to theologian Andrew Blosser.

Just wage: what makes a wage just in **Catholic social teaching** is not simply that the employer and employee both agree to it, but that the wage can support a worker and their family to a reasonable standard of comfort. See also **family wage**, **living wage**.

Latifundia: a Latin term for large privately owned farms, used in **CST** to flag a common situation of injustice when farmland becomes concentrated in the hands of a few wealthy owners. In the narrow set of circumstances where such concentration results in small farmers losing their livelihood or farmland no longer being used for food production, CST calls for **expropriation**.

Leisure: a state of being, distinct from work, in which we celebrate reality and the gifts we have received from God, including the gift of ourselves. As described by philosopher Josef Pieper, leisure is unproductive and celebrates what is, while work is active and seeks to change what is.

Living wage: Living wage movements in the US typically advocate for wages high enough to support a worker in reasonable comfort without the need to rely on government assistance. **CST** supports this goal but would add that wages, whether from the **direct employer** or the **indirect employer**, should also support a worker's family.

Objective sense or dimension of work: the observable ways our work changes the world around us; what the worker actually does and what results from it, such as things produced, created, changed, or maintained.

Reproductive labor: work that reproduces human bodies or communities, must be repeated constantly to achieve its purpose, such as food preparation or caregiving, and is distinct from "productive labor" such as building or manufacturing.

Sabbath: in the Jewish and Christian religious traditions, a day every week intentionally set aside to refrain from work, to rest, and to spend time with God.

Sacramental: in Catholic theology, sacraments use elements of **creation** to communicate spiritual realities to humans, such as Baptism, which uses water to symbolize and bring about a new relationship with God. Ordinary things can be **sacramental** when we recognize a greater reality communicated through a material thing, like the worker's creative ability present when we benefit from the products of her work.

Sin: in Christian theology, actions or states of mind that are opposed to God's plan for humanity.

Solidarity: recognizing that our interests are aligned with the interests of all other people and committing to live in light of that reality.

Stress cycle: a physiological reaction to stress that needs to be "completed" to restore the body to a sense of equilibrium.

Subjective sense or dimension of work: the way work changes the one who does it, as we either develop and enhance our skills and humanity, or become transformed in negative ways through our work tasks or working conditions.

Subsidiarity: the **CST** position that problems should be solved at the most appropriate level of authority. Those closer to the problem might understand the best way to solve it but may need help from more powerful or remote levels of authority to carry out their solution.

Total work: the cultural insistence that things, and people, are only valuable if and to the extent that they are economically productive, from philosopher Josef Pieper. See also **grind culture**; **workism**.

Universal basic income: a proposal to support workers' income and compensate people who do unpaid work by providing a basic cash income to every member of a community, usually envisioned as being provided by the government and funded through taxes. Recent **Catholic social teaching** sees it as a promising path to a **just wage**.

Universal destination of goods: the traditional Catholic belief that God created the good things of the earth for the purpose of serving the needs of all humanity, and this original, universal purpose outweighs any other property rights.

Vocation: means calling; Christians believe all humans are called to live out their relationship with God in a particular way that is unique to each person. Some see their paid work as their vocation, but vocation is best understood as greater than any individual job.

Work: see **inclusive definition of work**

Workism: a "new religion" defined by author Derek Thompson that sees work as the key to identity and human purpose at the individual level and to solving any problems of human suffering at the community level. See also **grind culture**; **total work.**

Index

acedia 98, 154
Agoro, Adebisi 104–108, 117n34
agricultural work. *See* farm work
ALICE (Asset Limited, Income Constrained, Employed) 127–129
alienating work 32–36, 38, 124–5, 153
   in sociology 57–58
American Compass 56, 128–9
Amoris Laetitia 44–45, 134
Annett, Anthony 90n33
artmaking
   and downtime 108–9
   as therapeutic 106–7
   as work 103–10

Bailey, James 136
Bailey, Matthew 104, 106, 107, 109, 117n36
Barrera, Albino 81
basic income. *See* universal basic income
Baum, Gregory 33
Beaudoin, Tom 86
Benedict XVI 39n9, 122, 123, 130, 147
Blosser, Andrew 110, 114
burnout 4–5, 25, 33–4, 68–9, 82, 112–13

care work
   economic value of 53–56
   low status of 21, 50–2
   for ourselves 46
   paid 55, 58n1
   as skilled labor 45–50
   undervalued 50–52
   unpaid 14–15, 20–1, 23, 28–30, 39n9, 41–58
   and women 28–30, 39n9, 43–4, 46–7, 50–1, 57–8
Caritas in Veritate 122, 123, 125, 130, 131, 147
Catholic social teaching
   authority of 2–3, 11–14, 17n16
   as a genre 10–14
   inclusive definition of work 6, 14, 16, 19–21, 28–9, 38, 41–2, 87, 155–6
   private property in 37, 74–8
   view of the human person 6–10, 14, 23–4, 32–3, 37, 51–2 (*see also* human nature)
   on women 28–30, 59n6, 133–4
Cavanaugh, William 83, 86
Centesimus Annus 31, 33, 122, 130, 144, 145, 147
child labor 29, 122, 134, 145
Clifton, Shane 52
Cloutier, David 86
Coalition of Immokalee Workers 82, 147
common good 33, 101, 136, 152
Compendium of the Social Doctrine of the Church 11, 20, 35, 127, 135, 137

Conferencia del Episcopado Mexicano 124
connective labor 49
Copeland, M. Shawn 7
Covid-19 pandemic 6, 42, 54, 63–4, 113–14, 149
 essential workers in 64, 80, 113–14
 inspiring new perspectives on work 6, 42, 113–14
Cox, Kathy Lilla 117n41
Crawford, Matthew 40n15, 71–2
creation 20–21
 sacramental view toward 84–87
 work as transforming 20–21, 24–5, 29, 70–4, 84–8
Criado Perez, Caroline 39n11
Csikszentmihalyi, Mihaly 65–67, 98–9, 117n32
CST. *See* Catholic social teaching

Day, Dorothy 83
Del Mastro, Addison 84
Detert, Rachel 90n23
Dies Domini 111
dignity. *See* human dignity
direct employer 123, 125, 134, 146–8
Doak, Mary 52
"doing nothing" 101–102, 110, 154

economic coercion 35, 120–1
embodiment 7
emotional labor 47–48, 58
encyclicals 10–14
Evangelii Gaudium 123, 126
expropriation 74, 76–8, 90n39, 91n45

Familiaris Consortio 44, 135
family grants 134–135, 145, 147
family wage 120, 131–7
farm work 64, 73–80, 82, 85–6, 91n45, 126, 150

Filipowicz, Matthew 104, 105, 117n37
Finn, Daniel 39n8, 92n62, 120, 132
flow 65–68, 70, 72, 83–4, 98–100, 103, 109, 117n32
 definition 66
food work 63–88
 dangerous 64, 78–80
 women and 64–65, 82–3
Francis 6, 13, 39n9, 44, 72, 77, 85, 112–14, 120, 123, 126, 135, 152
Fraser, Nancy 54
Fratelli Tutti 123, 126, 152
Friedan, Betty 35
Friedman, Milton 138n1
Fuerst, Ilyse Morgenstein 9

Garbes, Angela 45–47, 50
Garcia, Nick 104, 105, 108, 117n35
Gaudium et Spes 4, 8, 11, 27, 36–8, 74, 76, 77, 121, 125
gender. *See* women
Goldin, Claudia 7
Goodwin, Megan 9
Government Accountability Office, U.S. 145
Green, Alison 153
"grind culture" 100, 102
Guendelsberger, Emily 79

Hartman, Laura 86
Hersey, Tricia 100–103, 110
Hinze, Christine Firer 46, 50, 53, 55, 56, 58n1, 59n5–6, 98, 113, 133
Hochschild, Arlie Russell 42, 47–8, 52, 57
human dignity
 in Catholic social teaching 5, 8, 20, 52, 85–6, 111–12, 114, 131–2, 135
 challenges to 31–36, 78–81, 120–30

human nature   8, 12, 26, 32–3, 35–8, 131, 150

inclusive definition of work, in Catholic social teaching   6, 14, 16, 19–21, 28–9, 38, 41–2, 87, 155–6
indirect employer   80–82, 86, 88, 121–3, 146
inoperativity   110–113

Jaffe, Sarah   4, 5, 152
John Paul II   12, 21–2, 24, 37–8, 39n9, 43–4, 52, 67, 77, 111, 121–2, 126, 134–5, 144, 147, 152
Johnson, Rebecca May   71–72
just wage   119–121, 132–6, 145–8. *See also* living wage

Kelly, Conor   99

Laborem Exercens   20–24, 28, 35, 37–8, 43–4, 59n6, 70–2, 74, 80, 91n40, 111, 121, 124, 126, 134, 137, 149–50
   historical context of   24
labor unions. *See* unions
Lapp, Amber   56, 134
latifundia   74–79
Laudato Si'   13, 36, 72, 112, 143
leisure   95–103, 110–15, 153–4, 156
   vs. work   97–100
Leo XIII   21, 26, 29–30, 37, 38n3, 43, 74, 120–1, 131–2, 136, 144, 148
Lewandowski, Tom   152
living wage   131–133, 148
Luther, Martin   3–4, 27

Malesic, Jonathan   4, 5, 112
manual labor   70–73, 83, 109
Marx de Salcedo, Anastacia   82
Massaro, Thomas   39n8
Massingale, Bryan   151

Mater et Magistra   111, 125, 132
McMillan, Tracie   79
migrants, migration   12, 50, 60n27, 80, 123–4
moral injury   125

Nagoski, Amelia   68–69
Nagoski, Emily   68–69
Neujahr, Matthew   17n8
Noonan, John Jr.   18n16

objective dimension of work   21–25, 28
Odell, Jenny   100–103, 110

Pachirat, Timothy   79
paid work   20–21, 28, 53, 104, 106, 124–34, 136–7, 145–9
Parkes, Heidi   106–107, 109, 117n40
Paul, Dwayne David   36
Paul VI   77, 123
Perelman, Deb   65–67, 84
Petersen, Anne Helen   4, 5, 113
Pieper, Josef   96–103, 108–12, 115, 115n1
Pius XI   43, 125, 133
Pontifical Council for Justice and Peace   77, 135
Populorum Progressio   91n40, 122, 123
poverty   74, 76, 114, 123, 126–9, 136
   working   79, 126–9, 144
Powell, Mike   84
prison labor   34–36
private property, in Catholic social teaching   37, 74–8
Protestant work ethic   3
Pugh, Alison   49

Quadragesimo Anno   13, 29, 39n9, 43, 111, 125, 133, 145

racism   34–35, 50, 60n27, 76, 79, 80
reproductive labor   54, 56, 61n41, 64, 82, 84

Index

Rerum Novarum 21, 26, 29, 30, 37, 38n3, 39n9, 43, 74, 110, 120, 131, 133, 136, 144, 150
rest 36–37, 112–13
   vs. leisure 97–98
   as resistance 100–102, 110
   rest-amid and rest-apart 98–99, 109, 113
   right to 112, 137, 150
retirement 37–38, 137, 146, 149
Ross, Susan 84
Ryan, John A. 120, 131, 132

Sabbath 37, 110–12, 154
sacramentality 7, 84–7
Sandberg, Sheryl 57
Saracino, Michele 52
Sargeant, Leah Libresco 53
sex work 34, 150
sharecropping 76, 81
Shire, Warsan 124
Sieger, Anja Notanja 103–109, 117n33
sin 26, 98
slavery 31, 34, 121
Smith, Adam 24
solidarity 36, 86, 151–6
Sollicitudo Rei Socialis 126, 149, 152
Strauss, Elissa 50
stress cycle 68–69, 83–4, 153, 155
subjective dimension of work 21–25, 33, 36, 50
subsidiarity 87, 145
synods, in the Catholic context 59n7

Tablan, Ferdinand 32, 34
Thompson, Derek 2
Tyagi, Amelia Warren 129–130

U.S. Conference of Catholic Bishops 39n8, 78, 85, 124

unemployment 8–9, 23, 126, 130, 144–5
unions 6, 81–2, 113, 130, 136, 144–6, 149–51, 157
United Farm Workers 82, 150
United Nations 122, 148
United Way 127
universal basic income 110, 113–15, 118n54, 135–7, 145, 155
unpaid work 6, 19–21, 25, 29, 35, 41–58, 63–5, 69, 82–4, 102–10, 133–6, 153, 155–6
USCCB. *See* U.S. Conference of Catholic Bishops

Vatican Council II 11, 27, 37, 76–7, 121
vocation 3–5, 27–8, 104–5, 107, 155

wages. *See* just wages; work, paid
Wages for Housework 53–54, 56, 61n38
Warren, Elizabeth 129–130
Weber, Max 3
welfare 28, 39n10, 133–4, 146
Wilson, Katherine 151
women
   care work and 28–30, 39n9, 39n11, 43–4, 46–7, 50–1, 57–8
   Catholic social teaching on 28–30, 59n6, 133–4
   discrimination against, in paid work 24, 29–30, 50, 153
   food work and 64–65, 82–3
   paid work and 128–130, 132–4
work. *See also* alienating work; care work; child labor; farm work; food work; inclusive definition of work; manual labor; objective dimension of work; paid work; prison labor; sex

work; subjective dimension of work; unpaid work; workers' rights
  artmaking as   103–10
  bad work   31–36
  as a duty   28–31
  good for humans   26–28, 36, 66–73, 106–7, 149–53
  vs. leisure   97–100
workers' rights   36–38, 44, 78–9, 112, 121–37. *See also* just wage; living wage; rest; retirement
  direct employers and   35, 78, 147–8
  government's role in defending   37, 79–82, 144–7
  health care   126–129, 137, 146, 148–9
  indirect employer and   80–82
  right to form unions   10, 78, 130, 145, 149
  right to strike   150–51
  unions' role in defending   6, 81–2, 113, 130, 132, 146–7, 149–53
  workers' role in defending   35, 57–8, 149–54
"workism"   2–3, 5–9, 155

Žabić, Snežana   105–108, 117n38